Illinois

OFF THE BEATEN PATH™

"Excitement-seeking individuals and beleaguered parents, take heart. Rod Fensom and Julie Foreman have the answer to the question 'What are we going to do today?' In their book *Illinois: Off the Beaten Path*, Fensom and Foreman identify more than 500 unconventional things to do and see in your hometown and across the state."
—The *Herald*, Bourbonnais, Ill.

"If you're a typical tourist, you won't need the book. But if you look for something different when traveling around the state, this guide . . . describes, county by county, unusual museums, country inns, festivals and other unusual places and activities."
—*Outdoor Highlights*

"This book reminds us that this most midwestern of states has a surprising variety of interesting and unusual places to visit."
—*Innsider*

"It's a wonderful publication with a wealth of information for those of us who live in Illinois and for those just visiting as well. It's a welcome addition to our stock."
—Lincoln's New Salem Book Shop, Petersburg, Ill.

"*Illinois: Off the Beaten Path* lives up to its ambitious goals. The listings are comprehensive, readable and idiosyncratic . . . Belongs on the bookshelf—or better, in the glove compartment—of anyone with a serious itch to explore Illinois."
—*State Journal-Register*, Springfield, Ill.

OFF THE BEATEN PATH SERIES

Illinois

OFF <u>THE</u> BEATEN PATH™

FOURTH EDITION

ROD FENSOM
AND
JULIE FOREMAN

A Voyager Book

The Globe Pequot Press

Old Saybrook, Connecticut

Library of Congress Cataloging-in-Publication Data
Fensom, Rod
    Illinois : off the beaten path / by Rod Fensom and Julie Foreman.
    — 4th ed.
      p. cm. — (Off the beaten path series)
    "A Voyager book."
    Includes index.
    ISBN 1-56440-884-1
    1. Illinois—Guidebooks. I. Foreman, Julie, 1954– II. Title.
    III. Series.
F539.3.F46 1996
917.7304'43—dc20   96-5071
                                                   CIP

Manufactured in the United States of America
Fourth Edition/First Printing

ACKNOWLEDGMENTS

The authors would like to thank the Illinois Office of Tourism, chambers of commerce throughout Illinois, and a helpful group of correspondents from around the state who contributed a remarkable amount of information on places, sights, and attractions here in the Land of Lincoln.

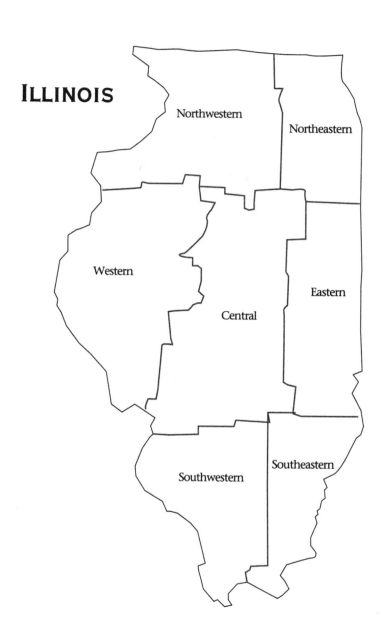

ILLINOIS

Northwestern

Northeastern

Western

Eastern

Central

Southwestern

Southeastern

CONTENTS

The prices and rates listed in this guidebook were confirmed at press time. We recommend, however, that you call establishments before traveling to obtain current information.

INTRODUCTION

Trips come in all kinds of boxes. There's the big one you open only once in a lifetime . . . a trip to China, for example. Some are neatly done up, thoughtfully planned, all tied together with a tidy bow—the standard-issue European motorcoach tour. But, as they say, good things come in small packages, too.

That's what we're about here, small packages, weekend trips and family vacations right here in our own backyard. What we've sought out, as the title says, are places off the beaten path. We like to think of them as surprises—perfect little jewel boxes that you turn over and over and examine closely—fascinating places filled with unexpected delights you probably wouldn't otherwise come across. Like us, if you're curious, a turner-down-of-back-roads, more than a little inquisitive, given to snooping into things, then you'll enjoy our county-by-county exploration of Illinois. If you don't need a Disneyland or a Las Vegas, you'll come along happily on our statewide travels. We've included a little bit of everything—a French fort, a two-story outhouse, fishing lakes and campgrounds, historic bits and corners, a golden pyramid and dancing horses. We've written about heavenly country cafes where biscuits and gravy scuttle even the most serious of diets. We've found country inns and guesthouses and even a few farms that welcome city vacationers. What we haven't included are Chicago and Springfield (places decidedly *on* the path), for a number of good guides to those cities exist.

For the not-so-easily persuaded, there's a lot more to Illinois than cornfields and Lincoln. But we're proud of both. Geographically, the state is crisscrossed by waterways, once thoroughfares of commerce, now recreation spots. Along the western border and in the south, the state turns hilly. While we may be the Prairie State, we have mountains and woodlands, as well. The Shawnee National Forest forms a green belt across the state's lower extremity, over the low mountains of the Illinois Ozarks.

When you use this guidebook, be sure to plan ahead. Check those attractions you want to visit, because hours and prices change frequently. When you're traveling through the state, ask. We've found the people to be universally friendly and helpful. What's more, we've discovered it's a pretty nice state, one rich in history and architecture, with a wealth of things to see and do—many free. So why not pack up the family and head out on a vacation in your own backyard. For a week or a weekend, there's something unexpected in Illinois.

NORTHEASTERN ILLINOIS

1. Illinois Beach State Park
2. Six Flags Great America
3. Ravinia Park Music Festival
4. Wauconda Orchards
5. Illinois Railway Museum
6. Woodstock Opera House
7. Anderson's Homemade Candies
8. Moraine Hills State Park
9. Morton Arboretum
10. Old Naper Settlement
11. Cantigny
12. Willowbrook Wildlife Haven
13. Paramount Arts Centre
14. Mooseheart
15. Fermilab
16. Garfield Farm and Tavern Museum
17. Fox River Trolley Museum
18. Santa's Village
19. Eberly's Honey Hill Apiaries
20. Rialto Square Theatre
21. Will County Historical Society Museum
22. Frankfort Historic District
23. Schutten-Aldrich House
24. Gebhard Woods State Park
25. Bradley House
26. Strickler Planetarium
27. Momence Gladiolus Festival

Northeastern Illinois

North Suburban Chicagoland

The character of Lake County changes at about the halfway point—from a collection of commuter bedroom communities to rural Illinois. At its lower edge are a number of the Chicago area's most affluent suburbs, such as Highland Park, Lake Forest, Deerfield, and Barrington. The county even claims the second greatest buying power in the United States at $34,428 per household average. At its northern border lies Wisconsin, and to the east, Lake Michigan. Other lakes, too, are never far away; there are more than 120 fishing and boating lakes in the county, including **Chain O'Lakes State Park.** Open year-round, the park has 220 campsites—some with electric hookup—showers, boat rental, fishing, and a playground. Go hunting from November to mid-December and horseback riding from May 1 to October. Snowmobiling and cross-country skiing are popular during the winter months. At 39947 N. State Park Road, Spring Grove 60081; (708) 587-5512.

◆ **Illinois Beach State Park** is only 20 miles east of Chain O'Lakes on Lake Michigan at Zion. The park's primary feature is a 7-mile stretch of beach with Illinois's last and best natural lakeshore dunes area.

Appropriate to its name, Zion hosts the **Zion Passion Play** each year at the Christian Arts Auditorium. Performances are scheduled in April and May and on Good Friday. Tickets are $9.00 for adults and $7.00 for students and senior citizens; (708) 746-2221.

In Libertyville is a very special place called **The Lambs** (Route 176, east of I-94). It is a nonprofit organization dedicated to helping mentally handicapped adults. The Lambs is both a residence and a workplace where vocational training and employment are provided. More than 155 residents work in The Lambs's ten businesses at the sixty-three-acre farm. Each year, a quarter of a million people visit Lambs Farm for special events and to sample the products made by the residents. Shop at the pet shop housed in a turn-of-the-century barn, the thrift shop or country store, the silk screen shop, or Grandma's Bakery. Younger visitors can entertain themselves at the petting farm (*do* feed the animals) or the minigolf course. The possibilities for fun are endless: an ice cream parlor, carousel, pony rides, miniature train rides, and antique fire truck rides. One of the most popular of The Lambs's offerings is **The Country Inn,** a wonderful old-fashioned restaurant with hearty home cooking. Open daily for lunch at 11:00 A.M. Dinner is served Tuesday through Saturday until 8:30 P.M. On Sunday, brunch is served 10:30 A.M. to 2:30 P.M. Dinners range from $5.00 to $12.00. For reservations call (708) 362–5050.

Also in Libertyville is the **Dave Adler Cultural Center** at 1700 N. Milwaukee; (708) 367–0707. Adler, an architect, built this twenty-three-room house around 1920, and it is now home to art exhibits and occasional concerts, storytelling, and barn dances. The family's private dining room has been restored with original furnishings. Open year-round, Monday through Friday 9:00 A.M. to 4:00 P.M. and Saturday 9:30 A.M. to 4:00 P.M. Admission is free.

What was formerly the farm of Illinois's most political family, the Adlai Stevensons, is here in Libertyville as well, now part of the **Lake County Forest Preserve**.

Bigger than the herd at Vienna's famous Spanish Riding School, the stable of the handsome Lipizzan stallions at **Tempel Farms** is the country's largest, right here in Wadsworth, Illinois. Catch a rare demonstration of equine talent at the 6,000-acre farm. Performances are held from early July to late August. Dates and times vary, so call for information. Performances last an hour and fifteen minutes and are held regardless of the weather. Stick around after the show for a tour of the stables. No reserved seating, adults, $12.00; seniors, $10.00; children 4 to 12, $5.00; under 4, free. At 15280 Wadsworth Road; (708) 623–7272.

For nature lovers, the **Des Plaines River Wetlands Demonstration Project** in Wadsworth is a show of its own. A joint undertaking of the Lake County Forest Preserve District and the conservation organization, Open Lands Project, it's 450 acres of marshes that have been restored or created. Project Director Donald Hey calls it a "living laboratory" where botanists, water quality experts, and environmental engineers from universities across the country come to conduct research. It's open to the public as well for hiking, bird-watching, and nature study. Watch for beaver, muskrat, and the rare yellow-head blackbird, in addition to migrating waterfowl. Call (312) 922–0777 for more information. The project is at U.S. Highway 41 at Wadsworth Road.

Cleopatra's ghost! Also in Wadsworth is the unique **Gold**

Pyramid House. Built by contractor James Onan, the 55-foot, 24K gold-plated pyramid is probably one of the most unusual residences in Illinois, if not the country. With a 200-ton statue of Ramses II standing guard, the structure is protected, too, by a spring-fed moat. It's oriented to true north, as is its model, the Great Pyramid of Cheops in Egypt. It's open to the public only by reservation April through October. Call (708) 662–6666 for information. Take I–94 north to Route 132, exit eastbound to Dilley's Road, turn left.

Another family entertainment spot—one with plenty of "show biz"—is ❖ **Six Flags Great America** in Gurnee, the single most popular amusement theme park in Illinois. Bugs Bunny, musical stage reviews, and the world's biggest and fastest double racing wooden roller coaster bring families by the thousands each summer. Theme villages, 150 attractions, and plenty of entertainment and food make it a sure bet for a Lake County outing. Open weekends only from the end of April, then daily mid-May through Labor Day and on weekends only through mid-October. Opens 10:00 A.M., closes at varying times. Adults, $29.50; seniors, $14.75; children 4 to 10, $24.50; 3 and under, free. At

The Gold Pyramid House

Gurnee, on Grand Avenue (Route 132), 1 mile east of I–94. Just west of Great America is bargain central, **Gurnee Mills,** one of the country's largest outlet malls.

Long Grove (at Route 83 and Route 53 in the southern part of the county), they say, invites you to turn your watch back to yesteryear. The historic village was settled in the 1840s by a group of German farmers who found it much like their own Alsatian homeland. Even after World War I, they continued to speak Plattdeutsch and to tend their farms. The village grew up as a place for farmers to buy their supplies, weigh their milk, make their cheese at the cooperative, and have their horses shod. In 1847 they built a tiny church on a hill near town, where services are still held today.

Antiques seem to be everywhere you look in Long Grove now, with one of the best collections of shops anywhere. The **Long Grove Apple Haus** (708–634–0730) presses its own cider, makes heavenly apple butter and jam, and should be a definite stop. **Long Grove Confectionery** (708–634–0080), on the other hand, is famous for hand-dipped chocolates. Try a fat, juicy, chocolate-covered strawberry on for size.

Each summer, the acclaimed Chicago Symphony Orchestra migrates north to Highland Park, taking up residence in their summer home, the ◆ **Ravinia Park Music Festival.** Since 1916 the outdoor music festival has featured a wide variety of classical and popular programs, including renowned guest artists, ballet, and chamber music. Take a picnic and lie on the lawn for music under the stars. Call (312) 728–4642 for reservations and prices. Late June through mid-September.

Settled in 1835, Waukegan has a rich history well worth exploring. Originally an Indian village and then a French trading post, its name means "Little Fort" in the local Indian dialect. In 1860 Lincoln, interrupted by fire, delivered what came to be known as his "unfinished speech" here. Today a bit of that past remains in **Old Waukegan,** a designated Historic District along North Avenue and Franklin Street. For more history the **Waukegan Historical Society,** 1917 N. Sheridan Road, is open Wednesday through Friday 10:00 A.M. to 2:30 P.M.; (708) 336–1859.

At 414 N. Sheridan Road, the white-pillared Greek Revival structure is home to the Lake County Chamber of Commerce. Built in 1847 by carriage maker John Swartout, the house is in the National Register of Historic Places.

5

If fishing is more to your taste, Waukegan is one of the two main Illinois ports for charter boats. Call (708) BIG-FISH for information on day trips for chinook and coho salmon. In June the city sponsors a **Coho Fishing Derby** with daily prizes. Just south of Waukegan and North Chicago is the **Great Lakes Naval Training Center,** Sheridan Road at Route 137. This 1,600-acre installation is the Navy's largest training center, even though it's 1,000 miles from saltwater. There are no tours, but most Fridays a public graduation ceremony for recruits is held. Guests begin arriving at 8:30 A.M. Call (708) 688–2201.

In the Lakewood Forest Preserve, at Route 176 and Fairfield Road, you'll find the **Lake County Museum,** a "small gem" of a place, according to the *Pioneer Press*, with a surprising postcard collection. Numbering 1.5 million pieces from 1878 to 1975, the collection documents popular American history of the first half of the century. Some years in June the museum also stages a Civil War reenactment. Call for details. Open 11:00 A.M. to 4:30 P.M. Monday through Saturday and 1:00 to 4:30 P.M. Sunday. Admission is $2.00 for adults and $1.00 for ages 4 to 17. Mondays are free. Call (708) 526–7878.

At the western edge of the county, in the little town of Volo, U.S. Highway 12 and Route 120, the **Antique Auto Museum** has on display more than 150 classic motor cars. And if you're souvenir-minded, the showroom has mint condition, but expensive, classic autos for sale; (815) 385–3644. Hours are 10:00 A.M. to 5:00 P.M. daily. Admission is $3.50 for adults, $2.50 for seniors, and $1.50 for children.

One of the area's best pick-your-own fruit farms is ◆ **Wauconda Orchards** at 1201 Gossell Road in Wauconda, just east of U.S. Highway 12. During the late spring and summer, you might find black raspberries, red raspberries, strawberries, or a handful of apple varieties just waiting to be picked; or try their country store for souvenirs such as cider, cheese, and sausage. Call (708) 526–8553. The orchards are open 9:00 A.M. to 5:00 P.M. weekdays as well as weekends; 7:00 A.M. to 5:00 P.M. May through December.

NORTHWEST SUBURBAN CHICAGOLAND

The lucky people of Union—all 600 or so—have more to see and do than many in much larger towns. Fairly close to almost nothing, Union boasts three major museums, each with a busy calendar of special events, and a collection of antiques shops to suit every taste.

To start with, the **McHenry County Historical Museum** is right on Main Street (6422 Main Street) in the middle of town. The log cabin in the front yard makes it even more difficult to miss. The 1847 structure was built by Luke Gannon on a site 5 miles northeast of Huntley, in the southern part of the county, and donated to the museum in 1964 by the family. A program of pioneer exhibitions is held here during the season. The museum also houses a collection of nineteenth-century musical instruments, ladies' fashions and handiwork, a quilt collection, farm equipment, and Civil War memorabilia. An 1895 school building is part of the museum complex. Open May through October Tuesday through Friday from 1:00 to 4:00 P.M. and Sunday from 1:00 to 4:00 P.M. Admission, adults $3.00; seniors and children, $2.00. Call for information on specially scheduled events; (815) 923–2267.

Just around the corner and a bit east of town on Olson Road in the middle of cornfields is one of our most-recommended museums in northern Illinois, the ❖ **Illinois Railway Museum.** The reasons for its popularity are severalfold: The attraction pleases all senses. You can touch the solid, worn seats as you sit back and enjoy a short train ride. You can enjoy the tingle of excitement as the train bell rings and the whistle blows. And you can watch with loving affection, as most visitors do, as the old steam engine comes puffing into the station. The Railway Museum is a nonprofit organization run by volunteers, train buffs who love the thrill of classic locomotives as much as we do. And most important, the exhibit is someplace the whole family can find fun. It's open air, with plenty of places to go—fifty-six acres worth—cars to ride, noises to hear, and even a spot for picnics.

When is a train more than a train? Well, when it's one of the museum's 200 cars and locomotives, which include electric interurbans, streetcars, trolleys, diesels, Chicago elevated cars, and even a complete silver Burlington Zephyr streamliner. It's one of only two places in the state you can ride a steam engine. (The other's in Monticello.) One of the most exotic stars of the show is the Russian Decapod from the Frisco Railroad, built in 1917 by Baldwin for the czarist Russian government, but, due to a revolution, never delivered.

Dating from 1851, the depot originally served as the station in Marengo. Behind it are the gift shop and bookstore with a mountain of railroad lore. Throughout the summer are special events, such as the July 4th Trolley Pageant, Railroad Day, and Diesel Day. From Memorial Day to Labor Day, the museum is open daily 10:00 A.M. to 4:00 P.M. and 10:00 A.M. to 5:00 P.M. on weekends. In May, September, and October, it's open weekends only; in April openings are limited to Sundays. For a ride on the steam train, plan to visit on a summer weekend when the trains run hourly. Admission varies but includes unlimited rides; call (815) 923-2488.

South of town, at 8512 S. Union, is **Donley's Wild West Town.** It's like someone's attic—someone who collected almost everything. One of the country's largest antique phonograph collections can be found along with records, cylinders, and needles.

A nickelodeon shows movies throughout the day right around the corner from the "Street of Yesteryear," a collection of old-time shops. Outside, the town has its own saloon, blacksmith shop, and pioneer cabin. Desperadoes shoot it out daily during the summer months in a flashy gunfight show. And conveniently nearby is the gallows, a real Chicago version, from the old Cook County jail on Hubbard Street, still waiting for "Terrible Tommy" O'Connor, who escaped on December 11, 1921, four days before his scheduled execution, the last one by hanging in the state. To record your day in the past, make a date with the photography studio, where you can get dressed up in Victorian garb or Wild West attire and have a sepia-toned souvenir in a matter of minutes. But certainly the favorite activity for kids is panning for gold pyrite. Try it—strike it rich! And afterwards celebrate with a scoop at the ice cream parlor. Open daily May through August and weekends only in April, September, and October. Call for hours; (815) 923-2214. Admission, $7.00 adults; $5.00 children 3 to 11.

In the center of the county is Woodstock, the county seat, named after the Vermont town from which many of its early citizens came. In the center of the town is the square, not with a courthouse (which is off to one side), but with a handsome park complete with bandstand, spring house, and a statue dedicated to "the soldiers of 1861–65, in honor of our nation's defenders."

On one side of the brick-paved square is the ✦ **Woodstock Opera House,** an 1890 structure listed in the National Register

8

of Historic Places (121 Van Buren). With its tall tower and ornate interior, its style has been called "Steamboat Gothic." Paul Newman and Orson Welles, who attended school in Woodstock, began their careers here. A seasonal schedule of performances is offered; (815) 338–5300.

On the other side of the square is the former courthouse and jail where a number of Chicago characters, including Eugene Debs, were once held. A stone on the side of the courthouse tells us that all this is only 954 feet above sea level.

Driving north from the brick-paved square at Woodstock, take Route 47 to Hebron, where even the perennial optimism of the Chicago Cubs fans is outdone by the Hebron water tower, painted to resemble a basketball with the notice that *this* is the home of the 1952 State Champions.

Just east of Hebron on Route 173 is Richmond, only blocks south of the Wisconsin state line. The legendary antique village is chockablock with antiques shops of every description. Head first, though, for **Ed's,** 10321 Main Street; (815) 678–2911. Ed's is open Tuesday through Saturday 10:30 A.M. to 5:00 P.M. and Sunday noon to 5:00 P.M. Most shops in town are closed on Mondays. Whatever your weakness, chances are it will find you here—from oak furniture to primitives, from china dolls to Mrs. Anderson's heavenly homemade chocolates.

Since 1919 ❖ **Anderson's Homemade Candies,** 10301 Main Street, has been bringing them in for hand-dipped English toffees, meltaway fudge, and old-fashioned "candy bars" that are really chocolate-covered apricot, orange peel, pudding, or "krispy" rice. Open daily 9:00 A.M. to 5:00 P.M., Sunday noon to 5:00 P.M. Closed Monday and two weeks in January.

The town holds special exhibits, such as a quilt show and an art glass exhibit, throughout the summer months. The last weekend in August is "Richmond Round-Up Days," where local service clubs, aided by the village, put on a do over at the Community Church. Fill up on a bratwurst, roasted ears of corn fresh from the field, and slabs of roast beef. Call the Richmond Memorial Hall for more information; (815) 678–4040.

A moraine, according to Webster, is "a mass of rocks, gravel, sand . . . carried or deposited by a glacier." And that's exactly what you'll find at ❖ **Moraine Hills State Park,** 3 miles south of McHenry. **Lake Defiance,** in the park, was created by a chunk of glacier left to melt there. Unusual natural features include a leatherleaf bog—120 acres of floating sphagnum moss and leatherleaf surrounded by a moat of open water. The pike marsh contains the largest-known colony of pitcher plants in Illinois along with cattails and bullrushes. It's a protected nature preserve and, as such, attracts a rich variety of wildlife as well. Visitors will want to stop at the interpretive center, which explains the park's natural resources. The Pike Marsh Nature Trail features a floating boardwalk perfect for exploration of park plant life. All state parks are open year-round except Christmas and New Year's Day. Contact the Site Superintendent, 914 S. River Road, McHenry 60050; (813) 385–1624.

West Suburban Chicagoland

Of what are euphemistically known as the collar counties—those surrounding Cook—Du Page County is surely the white collar enclosing the beefy neck of Chicago, buttoned-down, starched, of oxford cloth. It's conservative, Republican, a place of manicured lawns and solid brick homes (a drive through one of the county's prettiest towns, Elmhurst, will convince you of that).

On its northeast corner Du Page County slices through O'Hare International Airport; on the south it encloses the Argonne National Laboratory; and on the west it bisects the grounds of the Fermi National Accelerator Laboratory, one of the world's largest particle accelerators, where scientists from around the world come to study quirks and quarks. There's a lot going on in the county.

The ✦ **Morton Arboretum** offers year-round escape to nature for harried city dwellers. One mile north of Lisle, at the Route 53 exit of the East-West Tollway (I–88), the garden encompasses 1,500 acres of plants and trees and shrubs. Thirteen miles of footpaths and interpretive trails provide a look at nature. Hours are 7:00 A.M. to 7:00 P.M. during daylight savings time, 7:00 A.M. to dusk or 5:00 P.M. after October 29. There is a $6.00 charge per car ($3.00 on Wednesday). The arboretum has a delightful restaurant, **The Gingko,** open for lunch and tea daily (lunch ranges from $5.00 to $7.00), and a gift shop (708) 968–0074.

For history buffs, visiting the ✦ **Old Naper Settlement,** at 201 W. Porter in Naperville (708–420–6010) makes an ideal afternoon. Here, twenty historic buildings on a twelve-acre site re-create a nineteenth-century village. Costumed guides lead visitors through an assortment of structures: a windmill, barn, print shop, blacksmith shop, post office, smokehouse, and the tiny **Gothic Century Memorial Chapel.** The **Caroline Martin-Mitchell Mansion,** built in 1883, is listed in the National Register of Historic Places. Open May through October, 10:00 A.M. to 4:00 P.M. Tuesday through Saturday and 1:00 to 4:00 P.M. Sunday. Admission is $5.00 for adults, $3.00 for children ages 6 to 17. There is also an economical family rate of $13.00 for mom, dad, and the kids.

Furthermore, the **Old Graue Mill** at York and Spring Roads in Oak Brook is grist for a nostalgic afternoon. It's the only operating waterwheel in the state, and a white-aproned miller turns out stone-ground cornmeal for sale in the country store. At five pounds for $6.00, it's a bargain. Upstairs are a Victorian drawing room, kitchen, and children's room with antique dolls and toys, plus exhibits of spinning and weaving. Visit the new exhibit commemorating this stop on the historic Underground Railroad. Open 10:00 A.M. to 4:30 P.M. daily mid-April to mid-November; (708) 655–2090. Admission, $2.50 adults, $1.00 children, and $2.00 seniors.

Wheaton, the county seat, is home to **Wheaton College,** founded in 1853, and the headquarters of a number of religious publishing houses and organizations. Wheaton College is Billy Graham's alma mater and the site of the **Billy Graham Center Museum** with its Walk Through the Gospel and scenes from American evangelism since 1702. Temporary exhibits change quarterly. Open Monday through Saturday, 9:30 A.M. to 5:30 P.M., Sunday 1:00 to 5:00 P.M.; (708) 752–5909.

Not every county has its own mastodon, but at Armerding Hall on campus, a skeleton of the giant **Perry Mastodon,** which was found locally, is on exhibit; (708) 752–5010.

One of Wheaton's most famous sons is football hero Red Grange. At the **Red Grange Museum/Heritage Gallery,** 421 County Farm Road, displays and films tell the story of his life. Open Monday through Friday 8:00 A.M. to 4:30 P.M.

Also in Wheaton is ◆ **Cantigny,** the former estate of the late Colonel Robert R. McCormick, celebrated publisher of the *Chicago Tribune.* Today the 500-acre grounds are open to the public from 9:00 A.M. to sunset daily. Picnicking and walks through the formal gardens are popular pastimes. On Sundays at 3:00 P.M.

from May through August, outdoor concerts are held. The **First Infantry Division Museum** here commemorates the division in which the colonel served in World War I. At 15151 Winfield Road; (708) 668–5161. Admission is free, but there is a $5.00 parking fee; guided tours of the mansion are available. Open 10:00 A.M. to 5:00 P.M. daily except Monday during the summer months; 10:00 A.M. to 4:00 P.M. after Labor Day. The museum is closed during the month of January.

Another free and worthwhile Wheaton attraction is the **Du Page County Historical Museum,** located in an 1891 Romanesque-style limestone structure. Visit the special interactive gallery, which is popular with families, the Victorian period room, and the permanent collection of Du Page history. Little girls who "dress up" will love the historical costume gallery. Here, too, is almost a half mile of model railroad track. Watch trains chug along each third Saturday of the month from 1:30 to 3:30 P.M. At 102 E. Wesley Street; (708) 682–7343. Its hours are 10:00 A.M. to 4:00 P.M. on Monday, Wednesday, Friday, and Saturday and 1:00 to 4:00 P.M. on Sunday. Du Page County, in fact, has no shortage of museums—over a dozen in all.

Equally numerous are golf courses, if history's not your game. Du Page boasts twenty-four public courses, plus a handful of private courses, making it one of the most golf-accessible counties in the state. This mania is no recent phenomenon. The Chicago Golf Club, a private club in Wheaton, claims to have been the first eighteen-hole course in the United States, having opened in 1892.

Plenty of other outdoor activities are available in Du Page County, as well. For example, if your interests are somewhat patrician, there are polo matches each Sunday afternoon at 1:00 and 3:00 P.M. during the summer and fall at the **Oak Brook Polo Club,** York Road at Thirty-first Street in Oak Brook; (708) 990–2394.

During mid-May Lombard is abloom for the annual **Lilac Festival,** making it one of the best-smelling towns in the county. Parades are scheduled and a Lilac Queen is named. Call (708) 629–3799 for more information.

Especially pleasant is the **Illinois Prairie Path,** beginning in Elmhurst at York Road south of North Avenue. This 55-mile-long biking and hiking trail follows an old railroad right-of-way, where wildflowers, prairie grasses, tiny parks, and rest stops are plentiful. Call the highway department at (708) 682–7318 for a free map.

At Glen Ellyn, the ❧ **Willowbrook Wildlife Haven,** 525 S. Park Boulevard, is always popular with children. Here, wounded, lost, and captured native wildlife are cared for. Take a self-guided tour and visit the **Touch & Feel Museum.** The haven's hours are from 9:00 A.M. to 5:00 P.M. daily; (708) 790–4900, extension 245. Admission is free.

The county's forest preserves are among the finest in the area, with thirty preserves encompassing 17,500 acres. At various locations you'll find dog training fields, model airplane runs, bird-watching facilities, cross-country skiing, ice skating, hiking, and equestrian fields.

Oak Brook Center, Twenty-second Street and Route 83, is one of the Chicago area's outstanding regional shopping centers with Marshall Field's, Saks Fifth Avenue, Nordstrom, and Neiman-Marcus as major tenants. More than a hundred shops and restaurants are laid out around a landscaped courtyard.

One man could be credited almost solely with the settlement of the Fox River Valley, although that was certainly not his intention. Chief Black Hawk of the Sauk Indians was among the least friendly of the Indian leaders in the area that is now Illinois. In the War of 1812, he sided with the British against the Americans. The encroachment of the white settlers on his traditional lands led to the tragic Black Hawk War of 1832 in which the Sauk and Fox tribes were virtually exterminated.

Soldiers returning east from this frontier battle spoke highly of the fertile land along the river. Thus communities sprang up beside the waterway, notably Geneva in 1833, as supply centers for area farms and pioneers traveling farther west.

For the weekend traveler on nothing more than a sightseeing excursion, a trip through the Kane County towns of the Fox River is richly rewarding. Follow Route 31 along the eastern edge of the county as it meanders along next to the Fox River. In the south begin with Aurora, one of the first major cities in the nation to light its streets with electricity (1881).

Here the best show in town is the ❧ **Paramount Arts Centre,** 23 E. Galena Boulevard. On an island in the Fox River, the stylish old art deco movie and vaudeville palace was built in 1931 by noted theater architects Rapp and Rapp as a romanticized version of Venice. A 70-foot cascade light marquee adorns the redbrick and terra-cotta exterior. The Paramount was restored in 1978 and protected in the National Register of Historic Places two years later. In the theater's early days, Charlie Chaplin and the Marx Brothers were headliners. Today there's a varied schedule of visiting entertainers. Call (708) 896–6666 for program information.

West of town on Galena Boulevard (and about 2½ miles west of Randall Road) is the Fox Valley Park District's **Blackberry Historical Farm-Village.** From what was once a dairy farm has been fashioned a unique park with a collection of rides and historic exhibits. It receives high marks as an ideal spot for family outings.

Pony rides and an antique carousel vie for junior riders. A miniature steam train, Old Engine #9, takes visitors around the sixty-acre park and Lake Gregory to an 1840 **Pioneer Farm.** A petting barn with barnyard animals, hay wagon rides, and a pioneer log cabin where craftspeople demonstrate frontier skills are part of the attraction.

Museums on the property exhibit early carriages, a one-room schoolhouse, and Victorian women's furnishings. Throughout the season special events, such as **Antique Auto Day, Chautauqua Sunday, Smithing Day,** and **Indian Summer Day,** are scheduled. Open daily 10:00 A.M. to 4:30 P.M. May to Labor Day, Friday, Saturday, and Sunday 10:00 A.M. to 4:00 P.M. Labor Day to mid–October. Admission, which includes all rides, is $6.50 for adults and $5.50 for children. Call (708) 892–1550.

Back in Aurora one of the most unusual museums in the Fox Valley is the **Grand Army of the Republic Hall and Museum,** 23 E. Downer (708) 897–7221. The castellated limestone building with a statue of a Civil War soldier on top was built in 1877 and is listed in the National Register of Historic Places. Cannons line the front yard of the museum, which looks something like a church. Inside, Civil War memorabilia are the focus of the collection. Open 1:00 to 4:00 P.M. Monday, Wednesday, and Friday.

Between North Aurora and Batavia on Route 31 lies one of the most unusual communities in the entire state. ◆ **Mooseheart** is a wonderful, warm place you're certain to want to visit. An orphanage for 270 boys and girls, it's also a self-contained community run entirely by the Loyal Order of Moose. On 1,300 acres are a dairy farm and garden, a post office and bank, a school, field house, and even a furniture shop for supplying the needs of the residents. Tours are offered by student guides seven days a week, 9:00 A.M. to 2:00 P.M.; (708) 859–2000.

North of Aurora in Batavia is ✦ **Fermilab,** one of the world's largest particle accelerators. A free self-guided tour is offered seven days a week from 8:30 A.M. to 5:00 P.M. for groups of ten or fewer. Included is a fascinating eighteen-minute video that explains the working of the research center. The tour begins on the fifteenth floor of the Robert Rathbun Wilson Hall, with a view out over the entire complex. Complete the tour in your car, driving through the Fermilab facility (no public access to buildings in this area). Keep an eye out for the center's buffalo herd, some sixty strong, a historical counterpoint to the high-tech activities of the laboratory. Phone (708) 840–3000.

Just down the road, at 14 N. Washington Avenue in Batavia, is the 1885 Alexander Grimes farmhouse. The lovely old Victorian is home to **The Savery Shops,** a collection of five dealers and artists. Open daily from 10:00 A.M. to 5:00 P.M. and Sunday from noon to 5:00 P.M.; (708) 879–6825.

Continuing north on Route 31, **Geneva** is the next stop. Its historic district is a bonanza of period architecture with more than 200 structures listed in the National Register of Historic Places. Geneva is the county seat, and the 1891 **Kane County Courthouse** is historically significant, with unique wrought-iron balconies gracing the first to the fourth interior floors. Also be sure to see the W.P.A. mural in the post office at 26 S. Third Street. Founded as a trading center, Geneva is still that, with dozens of charming shops.

One of the oldest annual festivals in the state, Geneva's **Swedish Days** is held each June to commemorate the area's Swedish heritage. Quilts, crafts, *rosemaling* (Swedish painted flower decoration on furniture), and an unforgettable Swedish buffet are part of the fun.

Although it might not be fair to the other towns along the way, we think **St. Charles** is the jewel of the Fox River. Here pretty wooded slopes fall away to the slow-running river where the **Fox River Trail** (a bicycle and walking path from St. Charles to Aurora and north to Elgin) hugs the water. It's the perfect walking town, bisected by a river, with plenty of shops and side streets to explore. It's nice to see a small town where things are going well, business is thriving, the economy healthy.

You come away with an almost Disney-like impression of a town where clean streets and smiling faces are part of the package.

Make sure to schedule a visit to St. Charles during August for the town's Living History Month, put on by the St. Charles Historical Museum. Over three weekends, it's a potluck of military events. There are Revolutionary War and Civil War reenactment/encampments, each with costumed participants, demonstrations, two battles daily, period music, and a living, working camp with tents and supplies. Call (708) 584–6967 for dates and information. Or, during the rest of the year, stop by the museum at 2 E. Main Street in town.

St. Charles's claim to fame is antiquing. **Giant Antique Markets I, II, and III** are dealer cooperatives with a remarkable collection of stuff under each roof.

On the first Sunday of each month and the Saturday afternoon preceding it, the **Kane County Flea Market** takes over the County Fairgrounds with 1,400 dealers on twenty-five acres, attracting fifteen to twenty thousand or so shoppers. It has been called the largest flea market in the world, perhaps rightly so. The market ignores the weather and never cancels. Its success is the work of Helen Robinson, a seventy-year-old grandmother who actively supervises the monthly operation, including three kitchens and eight food trailers to feed the bargain hunters. Located on Randall Road just south of Route 64; (708) 337–2251. Open 1:00 to 5:00 P.M. on Saturday and 7:00 A.M. to 4:00 P.M. on Sunday. Admission is $4.00; children under 12 are free. Free parking.

Shoppers, too, will enjoy the three restored areas in town—**Old St. Charles, Century Corners,** and **Fox Island Square,** designed around the original Howell factory brick chimney. Lunch is a welcome respite, and the choices of restaurants are numerous.

Be sure to visit the cozy **Old Church Inn,** 18 N. Fourth Street, which is just what it sounds like. Formerly St. Patrick's Catholic Church, the limestone structure was erected in 1851. Seating is in the original church pews. Owners Brent and Bonny Guynn have transformed the interior with stained glass and antiques into an airy country dining room. Try the Friday night fish fry with memorable clam chowder for $9.95. Apart from the fish fry, dinners range from $10.95 to $18.95. There is outside dining, weather permitting. Call (708) 584–7341 for reservations.

16

In the handsome old 1928 **Baker Hotel,** a National Register building, the oval Rainbow Room has a back-lit colored glass floor and a view of the river. The Moorish stucco interiors lead out onto a terrace with a gazebo that's perfect for photographing the waterfalls behind the hotel. At 100 W. Main Street; (708) 584–2100.

But to *really* get the feel of the river, you have to get out on it. And the best way to do that is a ride on the *St. Charles Belle* or the *Fox River Queen,* 132-passenger paddlewheelers. Adults, $4.50; children, $3.00. Mid-May through mid-October, the excursion boats leave from Potawatomie Park at 3:30 P.M. on weekdays and at 2:00, 3:00, and 4:00 P.M. on Saturdays and Sundays; also at 5:00 P.M. on Sunday. Call (708) 584–2334. Also in this hilly, tidy park north of downtown are a swimming pool, a miniature golf course, and tennis courts. Note that there is a parking fee in the park.

Professional entertainment in St. Charles is offered at the **Dellora A. Norris Cultural Arts Center,** 1040 Dunham Road, (708) 584–7200, and at Pheasant Run, a resort complex with dinner theater, a comedy club, and children's theater east of town on Route 64, (708) 584–6300. Both feature name entertainers and shows.

Just west of St. Charles in La Fox is the ✦ **Garfield Farm and Tavern Museum,** a living farm of the 1840s. Roosters wander in and out of the weathered barns. Herbs and flowers grow in the curator's garden. In 1841 Timothy and Harriet Frost Garfield brought their eight children from Vermont to the prairie lands of Illinois. In 1977 the third-generation owner, Elva Ruth Garfield, donated the farm as a museum; one of the most intact historical sites in the country, it is used for ongoing archaeological studies. It's the largest Illinois farm in the National Register of Historic Places, and it gives the visitor an excellent idea of just how a farm family of the 1840s must have lived. Walk through the grounds and the interior of the brick (made locally) home and tavern with curator Jerome Johnson and his wife, Holly. In early October the three-day **Fall Festival** features historical music, a storyteller, blacksmithing, craft demonstrations, and hearty farm cooking appropriate to the period. Open 1:00 to 4:00 P.M. on Wednesday and Sunday, June through September or by appointment. Adults, $3.00; children, $1.00. Call (708) 584–8485 for a schedule of seasonal events.

Farther north on Route 31, in South Elgin, is the ✦ **Fox River Trolley Museum,** where you can take a 3-mile, 30-minute ride along the Fox River on this electric railway. Vintage railway cars are on display. Open Sunday 11:00 A.M. to 5:00 P.M. May through early November, Saturdays 11:00 A.M. to 5:00 P.M. in July and August; (708) 697–4676. The museum is on Route 31 in South Elgin, 3 blocks south of State Street. Adults, $2.50; children, $1.50.

In Elgin don't go looking for the Elgin Watch Factory, since 1866 the manufacturer of America's best-known timepieces. It closed in 1965. What you can explore, however, is the **Elgin Historic District.** The National Register district includes 667 structures, many of noteworthy architecture—Greek Revival, Queen Anne, Shingle style, and brick row houses. Walking tour or bicycle tour maps are available from the Elgin Visitors Bureau; (708) 695–7540.

Another important industry for Elgin was the dairy business, and it was here that Gail Borden invented his process for condensing milk in 1856. Have lunch at **Focaccia's,** a restaurant located in the old Borden library on Spring Street in the heart of Elgin.

The **Dundee area,** just north of Elgin, claims its famous sons as well. Allan Pinkerton, famous detective and head of the Union Army's spy service in the Civil War, lived here from 1844 to 1850. A historical marker indicates the site on Third Street in West Dundee. Evangelist Billy Sunday owned the farm on which his wife was born in Sleepy Hollow, just west on Route 72.

In Dundee tour the family-owned **Haeger Potteries Factory** at 7 Maiden Lane. From the banks of the Fox River, the company founder took clay to use in his Dundee Brickyards in 1871 to make bricks that were used to rebuild Chicago after the Great Chicago Fire. Tours available Monday through Friday at 10:00 A.M. and 1:00 P.M., free; (708) 426–3441. Factory outlet open Monday through Friday, 8:30 A.M. to 5:00 P.M.; Saturday and Sunday, 10:00 A.M. to 5:00 P.M.

 Santa's Village, Route 25 and Route 72 in East Dundee, is a popular amusement park for children with a petting zoo; more than forty rides, shows, and attractions; and live shows at the Evergreen Theater. Open daily mid-June to Labor Day, weekends mid-May through September. September through April family skating's the thing at the Polar Dome Ice Rink ($4.75 per person). Hours are 10:00 A.M. to 6:00 P.M. weekdays, 11:00 A.M. to 6:00 P.M. weekends. Admission, $12.95; (708) 426–6751.

One of the Fox Valley's most popular restaurants, **The Milk**

Pail, is also located in East Dundee. The fifty-year-old family favorite features country cooking with specialties such as breast of pheasant, trout, duck, and fresh-baked goods. Dinners range from $7.95 to $16.95. At Route 25, open seven days a week; (708) 742–5040

In the northwest corner of the county is the town of Hampshire, home of ◆ **Eberly's Honey Hill Apiaries**—with 1,600 hives, the largest in Kane County. The retail shop sells clover, buckwheat, and wildflower honey in addition to beekeeping supplies and homemade beeswax candles. If you're not afraid of being stung, out back is abuzz with the busy little creatures. The apiary is located on U.S. Highway 20 in Hampshire; (708) 464–5165. Open 9:00 A.M. to 5:00 P.M., seven days a week.

SOUTH ENVIRONS OF CHICAGOLAND

Will County's seat, Joliet, may call to mind only the Blues Brothers and an infamous state prison (part of the movie was set here). But this community of 78,000, 40 miles southwest of Chicago, has numerous other, more pleasant features. For example, it's known as the City of Spires, for the 122 houses of worship that dot the area.

The temple of art, however, that attracts the cultural faithful from miles around is the old ◆ **Rialto Square Theatre,** "The Jewel of Joliet." Built in 1926 by the renowned theater designers Rapp and Rapp, this masterpiece is a remarkable example of theater baroque. Restored in 1981, it is in the National Register of Historic Places. Here, where Fanny Brice and Al Jolson once performed, a list of modern-day luminaries headlines the bill at the new performing arts center—Broadway shows, orchestras, singers, and comedians.

But in this palace for the people, the real show's before the show. You enter a block-long lobby lined with mirrors, its splendor compared to that of the Hall of Mirrors at Versailles. This lobby leads into the domed rotunda with bas-relief sculptures by Eugene Romeo. From the dome hangs the largest hand-cut chandelier in the United States, "The Duchess," 20 feet long with eight arms of copper and bronze and more than 250 lights. Beyond the rotunda is the auditorium, no less impressive. The twenty-one-rank Barton Grande Theatre Pipe Organ is a prized instrument that is used in occasional recitals at the Rialto. Tours are scheduled each Tuesday at 12:45 P.M. or by appointment; (815) 726–7171. Admission is $3.00. For performance information and tickets, call (815) 726–6600.

The city's historic districts are also worth inspection. The **South East Neighborhood Historic District,** south and east of downtown, is a Registered National Landmark District. The feature home is the opulent **Victorian Manor,** a three-story, forty-room Italian Renaissance mansion (at 20 S. Eastern Avenue, tours available). Just west of the Des Plaines River, on North Broadway and Hickory Streets, are splendid Second Empire-style homes and authentic examples of original Joliet limestone residences. Up the hill from downtown Joliet, west along Western Avenue, are turn-of-the-century Victorian mansions in all of their ornate glory.

Another reminder of this river city's historic past are the *Empress River Casino* boats. Fourteen times daily, seven days a week, two boats sail for two-hour gambling cruises. And while the idea is old-fashioned, the boats are sparklingly new—each a "contemporary mega-yacht" as the promotional material says. Try your hand at blackjack, roulette, craps, or the slots (for as little as 25 cents). There are snack shops on the boats and restaurants in the land-based pavilion. Call (708) 345–6789 for reservations and information. On the Des Plaines River, 3 miles southwest of downtown on Route 6.

Completed for the nation's bicentennial year for a lasting memorial, the **Bicentennial Park Theater and Bandshell** complex at Jefferson and Bluff Streets is home to an outdoor concert season and a beautiful 300-seat formal theater. Free weekly lawn concerts are offered each Thursday in June, July, and August. Call (815) 740–2216 for more information.

Joliet, named for Louis Joliet, who explored the area with Father Marquette in the 1600s, is home to the county's first junior college. The castellated stone structure, designed by noted architects Daniel Burnham and F. S. Allen in 1902, is today the central campus of **Joliet Township High School** at 201 S. Jefferson Street.

In the city's Highland Park is the **Greenhouse,** repository for an exceptional collection of exotic flora. Featured are cacti more than a hundred years old and seasonal flower shows.

An essential part of Joliet, as well as Will County as a whole (and Cook, La Salle, and Grundy counties), is the Illinois and

Michigan Canal. In 1984 it became the newest member of the National Park System, the **Illinois and Michigan Canal National Heritage Corridor,** running from Chicago to Peru, Illinois. It contains historic sites, residential neighborhoods, forest preserves for picnicking, fishing, hiking, canoeing, and camping, plus thirty-nine rare natural areas, remnants of the ancient Illinois landscape. Among them is the **Lockport Prairie** at Route 53 and Division Street, south of Route 7, across from Stateville Correctional Center. Some of the best examples of native prairie grasses and wildflowers still may be found there.

Now obsolete, the canal was once the principal transportation link connecting the Chicago and Illinois Rivers, providing a continuous waterway from the Atlantic Ocean through the Erie Canal, Great Lakes, and the Mississippi to the Gulf of Mexico. The I&M Canal, dug by hand between 1836 and 1848 over 96 miles, made possible the settling of the northern part of the state and the growth of the city of Chicago. Over it traveled immigrants from Sweden, Germany, and Ireland; cattle and goods; and the tools of settlement of the American westward movement. Settlement and industry followed the opening of the waterway, and with that, the growth of canal towns characterized by distinctive architecture.

One of the most picturesque is Lockport. History in Lockport is everywhere. The town was platted in 1836 by the I&M commissioners to serve as the headquarters for the canal. The headquarters building—in the National Register and part of the Lockport National Register Historic District—is now the ◆ **Will County Historical Society Museum**—crammed with artifacts of the canal period—at 803 S. State Street; (815) 838–5080. Free. Open daily 1:00 to 4:30 P.M. year-round.

Adjacent to the museum is the **Pioneer Settlement,** located along the banks of the canal at Eighth Street. In an open area once used by farmers to load their cargo onto canal boats, the historical society has created an open-air museum with historic buildings brought to the site from around the county. Included are a one-room schoolhouse, a blacksmith shop, an 1860s farmhouse, a jail, and an 1830s log cabin, the oldest building in the county. Open mid-April to early October. Free.

A 2½-mile trail follows the east bank of the canal through Lockport. Accessible year-round by hikers, joggers, bicyclists, and cross-country skiers, the trail is marked with interpretive signs explaining the history of the waterway. It crosses over old **Lock Number One,** where locally quarried stone walls remain. The trail terminates in **Dellwood Park,** originally built in the early 1900s by the Chicago Interurban Railroad as an amusement park. Today it boasts tennis courts, a swimming pool, floral gardens, ball fields, and a summer program of free concerts at the performing arts center.

A side note: Some of the county's earliest steel plows were first fashioned in Lockport by inventor John Lane in 1835. His plows, which shaped the face of Illinois agriculture, were manufactured at a site near Gougar Road and Seventh Street.

After an afternoon of history, a delightful counterpoint is **Tallgrass,** a decidedly gourmet restaurant, 1006 S. State Street, a place that's even been acclaimed by tough Chicago restaurant reviewers. Housed in what was once a barn used for I&M canal workers, the mood is elegant, the food epicurean, the prices steep.

Frankfort, forty-five minutes south of Chicago at U.S. Highway 30 and U.S. Highway 45, is known as the "town with 1890 charm." Listed on the Illinois Historic Landmark survey, the ◆ **Frankfort Historic District** contains many restored shops and homes typical of a nineteenth-century crossroads village. Today antique-hunters come from miles around for the village's growing collection of antiques shops. Most shops are closed on Monday. The Chamber of Commerce has further information, including walking maps and tours; (815) 469–3356. An annual fall festival is scheduled over Labor Day weekend. Visit, too, the **Frankfort Area Historical Society Museum** at Kansas and Hickory Streets, open Sunday 1:00 to 4:00 P.M.

In the southern part of the county, Wilmington is one of northern Illinois's most unusual towns. On the Kankakee River, it's known as the "Island City" because the river runs through downtown, forming an island home to two city parks, **North and South Island Parks.**

Architecturally significant is the ◆ **Schutten-Aldrich House**, 600 Water Street, a landmark octagonal residence built in 1856. The 1836 **Peter Stewart House,** at Kankakee and the Outer Drive, was an important stop on the Underground Railway in the years before the Civil War.

During most of the year, visitors come to Wilmington for the dozens of antiques shops in the area.

The Schutten-Aldrich House

The little village of New Lenox is home to two historically important buildings—the redbrick **tavern** (now a private residence) on the south side of U.S. Highway 30, just west of the New Lenox-Frankfort border, built prior to 1830 and used as a coach stop and tavern on the Joliet-LaPorte (Indiana) line; and the **Gougar residence** at Gougar Road and U.S. Highway 30, home of the first county postmaster. On the last Saturday in June, the village holds its **Old Campground Festival.**

Perhaps nothing demonstrates quite as eloquently the changes in our society as the juxtaposition of the historic and the futuristic. In Morris, the seat of Grundy County, the towering shapes of the Dresden Nuclear Power Station form a striking contrast to the waters of the old Illinois and Michigan (I&M) Canal, which flow past town and through ✦ **Gebhard Woods State Park.**

The thirty-acre park, named after its donor, Fred Gebhard, is

23

situated off Route 47 at the southwest edge of Morris on the north bank of the I&M Canal. The park has four ponds for children's fishing plus adult fishing in the canal and in Nettle Creek, which form the north and east boundaries of the park. Largemouth bass, bluegill, sunfish, and catfish are caught. With an impressive collection of shade trees—walnut, oak, cottonwood, ash, and maple—picnicking is a popular activity here. Gebhard Woods is part of the **I&M Canal State Trail** and the **I&M Canal National Heritage Corridor.** For further information contact the Site Superintendent, Gebhard Woods State Park, P.O. Box 272, Morris 60450; (815) 942–0796.

East of Morris, in **Evergreen Cemetery,** lies the grave of Shabbona (1775–1859), the chief of the Potawatomi tribe, who sided with the settlers during the Black Hawk War of 1832. Even though a proven friend, Shabbona and his tribe were forced to move to a reservation in Kansas in 1836. He later returned to Illinois. The city of Morris honors the Indian hero with one of the last working steam pump fire engines in the country. **Old Shab-a-nee,** in use from 1868 to 1922, still appears today in parades.

The last weekend in September, Morris hosts the **Grundy County Corn Festival,** one of the largest county agricultural festivals in the state. Parades, exhibits, musical concerts, and boat excursions on the Illinois River make it a perfect family outing. Call (815) 942-CORN for information.

About 8 miles southeast of Morris and south of the Illinois River is **Goose Lake Prairie State Park,** one of the last remnants of prairie left in this, the Prairie State, and one of the largest preserves in the tall grass region of North America. As such it has national significance. Of its 2,357 acres, 1,513 are dedicated as an Illinois Nature Preserve.

There is, however, no lake at Goose Lake, having been drained at the end of the last century for farming and for the clay deposits under it. Instead, the grasses and flowers are much like what the state's earliest settlers would have encountered. The palette of wildflowers changes in hue throughout the seasons: in spring the violet shooting star and blue-eyed grass; in summer false indigo and blazing star; and in fall aster and goldenrod.

The park's Tallgrass Nature Trail offers a fascinating walk through 1½ miles of prairie and across potholes, marshes, and a unique floating bridge.

A two-story replica of the 1834–35 **John Cragg cabin,** nicknamed the Palace, stands in the park. The original was a station on the Underground Railroad.

An interpretive program is offered year-round except winter weekends. The visitors center is open 10:00 A.M. to 4:00 P.M. The park's address, on Jugtown Road, comes from an early settlement here. Dating from 1853 Jugtown was a small community whose inhabitants made drain tiles, water jugs, and pottery from the region's clay. For information on the park, contact the Site Superintendent, 5010 N. Jugtown Road, Morris 60450; (815) 942–2899.

The Kankakee River, the namesake of the county and city, offers more than just scenic beauty. Six miles northwest of Kankakee on Route 102, along the river's banks, is the **Kankakee River State Park,** 2,780 wooded acres spread out along 11 miles of the river. The first European to travel down that river was Rene Robert Cavalier, Sieur de la Salle, who, with a party of fourteen men, traveled from the headwaters of the Kankakee down to the Illinois River in 1679.

Modern explorers make the trip downstream daily throughout the summer on one of the cleanest waterways in the state. **Reed's Canoe Trips,** 907 N. Indiana Avenue, Kankakee, books canoe trips from two hours to six hours and overnight, as well. Canoes, paddles, life jackets, and return transportation are provided. The service operates daily from April 1 to October 15; (815) 932–2663.

The state park's **Rock Creek Canyon** is especially pretty with its picturesque waterfall and gnarled cedars growing from its steep limestone walls. Hiking, equestrian, and snowmobile trails are laced throughout the park's forested acres. Picnic facilities and camping (with electric hookup) are available. Hunting and fishing are seasonal sports in the park. In the summer the park rangers present an informative interpretive program. For information contact the Park Ranger, R.R. 1, Bourbonnais 60914; (815) 933–1383.

Each July, anglers from around the Midwest gather to try their luck in the annual **Kankakee River Valley Fishing Derby.** More than $100,000 is awarded in prizes to those who land the tagged fish. For more information call (800) 747–4837 in Illinois, (815) 935–7390 outside the state.

Golf, too, has its proponents, and Kankakee County has the courses to satisfy even the most avid. There are seven courses, including the **Bon Vivant Country Club** (815–935–0403), ranked second in the district only after Butler National by the

Chicago District Golf Association.

During Labor Day weekend, the **Kankakee River Valley Regatta** brings powerboats to the river from miles around for fast and wonderful racing championships.

In the southwest part of Kankakee, at Eighth Avenue and Water Street, is the boyhood home of Len Small, twenty-eighth governor of Illinois. Situated on a twenty-two-acre park, the home is part of the **Kankakee Historical Society Museum.** The 1855 Italianate limestone building has been restored and rooms furnished in period style. On the grounds visitors can tour a historic one-room schoolhouse. Admission is free. Open year-round 9:30 A.M. to 4:30 P.M. Monday through Thursday and 1:00 to 4:00 P.M. on Saturday and Sunday. Call (815) 932–5279.

Kankakee's ◆ **Bradley House,** at Harrison and the river, was designed by Frank Lloyd Wright as a private residence, the first in his famous "Prairie style." The 1901 structure is true to form with long, low lines and overhanging eaves. Set in a grove of trees on the Kankakee River, the effect is a natural, harmonious one. Wright also designed the original furnishings, china, and rugs for the home. In 1953 the architectural showplace became a charming inn, run by two army cooks. It's private now and no longer open as a restaurant. Call the visitor's bureau for details: (800) 747–4837 in Illinois; (815) 935–7390 out of state.

Bourbonnais, just north of Kankakee, was one of the earliest settlements on the Kankakee, dating from the founding of a French trading post here in 1832. An influx of French Canadians followed, giving the region its French flavor. In Bourbonnais is the Olivet Nazarene University (formerly the Catholic St. Viator College), with its renowned ◆ **Strickler Planetarium;** (815) 939–5395. More than 4,800 stars are projected onto a 30-foot dome in a series of seasonal programs. Call for schedules and times. Admission is $1.00 for adults and children.

Momence, too, is a historic community, once known as the Old Border Town (between wilderness and civilization), situated on the Hubbard Trail linking Fort Dearborn (Chicago) to Vincennes, Indiana. The road, also known as the Vincennes Trail, was designated a state road, later Illinois 1.

Momence today boasts a number of historic homes. The **Momence Historic House,** 11 N. Dixie Highway, is a furnished home that lets the visitor see what life was like in the period 1870–1900. The kitchen, with its dry sink and pump, pie safe,

26

The Bradley House

and butter churn, speaks of a time without modern appliances. Open May through September, Saturday and Sunday only, 2:00 to 4:00 P.M. Free.

A major industry in the area is the growing of gladioli—more than 150,000 are harvested annually. In early August, the ◆ **Momence Gladiolus Festival** draws thousands from across the country. In addition to lovely flowers, there are parades, antique car shows, a flea market, an antique tractor show, and a family fun run. Call (815) 472–4620 for more information.

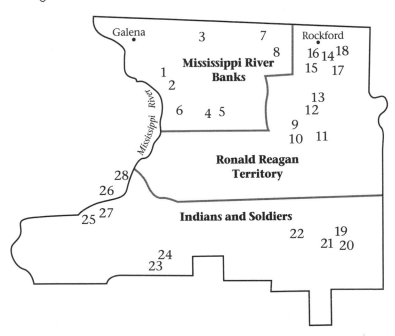

1. Ulysses S. Grant Home
2. Grant Hills Antique Auto Museum
3. Apple River Canyon State Park
4. Commercial Core
5. Campbell Center for Historic Preservation
6. Mississippi Palisades State Park
7. Civil War Monument
8. Freeport Art Museum/Arts Council
9. President Ronald Reagan Boyhood Home
10. Fort Dixon
11. Amboy Depot Museum
12. John Deere Historic Site
13. *Black Hawk*
14. Time Museum
15. Burpee Museum of Natural History
16. Tinker Swiss Village
17. Magic Waters
18. Rock Cut State Park
19. Reddick Mansion
20. Effigy Tumuli
21. Starved Rock State Park
22. Owen Lovejoy Homestead
23. Bishop Hill
24. Bjorklund Hotel
25. Rock Island Arsenal
26. Hauberg Indian Museum
27. Center for Belgian Culture
28. Niabi Zoo

Northwestern Illinois

Mississippi River Banks

The scenery along the Mississippi River, down into the Mississippi River Palisades State Park, is one of the prettiest and hilliest terrains in the state. Beginning at the northern corner of the state is Galena, the second-largest tourist attraction in Illinois (after Springfield). Although it wouldn't quite be considered "off the beaten path," so many small-town charms are here that it would be a mistake to overlook it.

Galena's life as a tourist attraction began about twenty years ago as a spot to spend the day, browse through a few quaint shops, hunt for antiques, and visit the home of General Ulysses S. Grant.

As an introduction to the town, the **Galena/Jo Daviess County History Museum,** 211 S. Bench Street, offers two thirty-minute self-guided walking tours. This is an excellent way to get your bearings and to decide at which places you will want to spend more time. The tours begin at the Chamber of Commerce office in the railroad depot at 101 Bouthillier Street, where you can pick up a map that takes you through the business and shopping district, about 6 blocks long.

There are a half dozen other guided tours available in Galena. Contact the Galena/Jo Daviess County Convention and Visitors Bureau, (800) 747–9377, 101 Bouthillier Street, Galena 61037 for a listing.

Galena's main attraction is the ♥ **Ulysses S. Grant Home.** It's not on the walking tour but is within walking distance from the Chamber of Commerce. Instead of heading west across the bridge, go east along Bouthillier Street and you'll run right into it, on the corner of Bouthillier and Fourth Streets. The house is open daily from 9:00 A.M. to 5:00 P.M., and admission is free.

There is also the guided **Galena History Tour,** which begins at the Galena/Jo Daviess County History Museum on Bench Street. See a slide-tape presentation and tour the museum. Next visit the General Store Museum, the historic downtown district, and Grant's home. The tour then travels through Grant Park, with its statue of the general, and recrosses the bridge to end at the 1845 Market House, where you see a slide presentation on Galena's architecture. For tour information contact the Galena/Jo

Daviess County History Museum, P.O. Box 18, Galena 61036; (815) 777-9129. The museum is open daily 9:00 A.M. to 5:00 P.M. year-round.

Another interesting stop in Galena is the **Fulton Brewery Market,** just west of the U.S. Highway 20 bridge at the corner of U.S. Highway 20 and Prospect Street. There are twelve retail shops in the building. It is open May 1 through October from 10:00 A.M. to 5:00 P.M. and from 10:00 A.M. to 5:00 P.M. November through April. The market is at 601 S. Prospect Street; (815) 777-1514.

The **Belvedere Tour Home,** Park Avenue, built in 1857, is one of Galena's largest mansions and has been restored and furnished with antiques. Other restored homes that are open to the public are the **John Dowling Stone House,** Diagonal Street, and the **Turney House,** U.S. Highway 20 West. The homes are open 10:00 A.M. to 5:00 P.M. daily.

Galena also has two **House Tours weekends,** the last full weekend in September and again in June, when you can view privately owned, restored homes, mansions, and cottages not usually available to the public.

The **Old Market House** is open 9:00 A.M. to noon, 1:00 to 5:00 P.M. daily, and admission is free. Inside in the Main Hall are wall panel photos, diagrams, and a short narrated slide show about architecture. The South Wing has a commerce and mining exhibit, and the basement has a mural collection of photos and printed documents of the Market House.

The ❖ **Grant Hills Antique Auto Museum** has antique, classic, and special interest automobiles of yesteryear on display. Hours are 10:00 A.M. to 5:00 P.M. daily during the summer and weekends 10:00 A.M. to 5:00 P.M. from November through May 15. No set schedule for the rest of the year, so call (815) 777-2115 for hours.

Galena Cellars Winery, 515 S. Main Street, (815) 777-3330, is just inside the Flood Gates on Galena's Main Street in a restored 1840s granary building. You'll enjoy watching the working of this operating winery. The family-owned business produces 8,000 cases a year, most sold at the winery. The forty-five minute tour includes wine tasting. Admission is $1.00, and the winery is open daily except major holidays. Call for tour times.

Galena boasts plenty of places to stay, and that includes resorts, hotels, and bed-and-breakfast establishments. The Chamber of Commerce and the Visitors and Convention Bureau have listings. Many of the guest houses and bed-and-breakfasts are in refurbished homes and are a delightful change from standard hotels.

For additional information you can contact the Chamber of Commerce, 101 Bouthillier Street, Galena 61036, (815) 777–0203 or 800–747–9377, or the Convention and Visitors Bureau, 330 N. Bench Street, Galena 61036, (815) 777–3357.

The **Galena Public Library & Historical Collection,** 529 S. Bench Street, (815) 777–0200, includes a mosaic fireplace in a wisteria pattern, done in the style of Frank Lloyd Wright. Among its other historic collections are Galena newspapers from 1834 to the present. Historical Collection hours are 1:00 to 8:30 P.M. Monday through Friday; 1:00 to 4:00 P.M. Saturday; or by appointment. Library hours are 1:00 to 6:00 P.M. Monday, Tuesday, Friday; 1:00 to 8:30 P.M. Wednesday; 9:00 A.M. to 6:00 P.M. Thursday and Saturday.

The **Galena Wax Museum,** 119 N. Main Street, (815) 777–3121, has a collection of thirty-two figures of historic characters and celebrities, including Grant and Lincoln. The tour lasts between fifteen and thirty minutes. Admission is $2.50 for adults, children $1.00, and under 5 free. Hours are 10:00 A.M. to 5:00 P.M. daily September through May, and 10:00 A.M. to 9:00 P.M. daily June, July, and August.

The **Old Stockade Refuge,** 208 Perry Street, (815) 777–1646, has Indian and pioneer history displays. The tour runs about thirty-five minutes and admission is $2.00 for adults; children 5 to 12, 75 cents; under 5, free. Hours vary, so call ahead.

Galena also offers river cruises. The *Julia Belle Swain,* (815) 777–1660, is a 115-passenger steam-driven sternwheeler. A two-day cruise on the Mississippi departs from LeClaire, Iowa, docks overnight near Galena, and returns to LeClaire. Reservations are required.

The **Jo Daviess County Riverboat Corporation,** (815) 777–2648, has casino cruises. There are four three-hour cruises daily. Call for details.

◆ **Apple River Canyon State Park** has 297 acres for picnicking, camping, fishing, hiking, and winter sport activities. Contact Apple River Canyon State Park, Apple River 61001; (815) 745–3302. From Warren drive 4 miles south on Route 78, then go 4 miles west on a county road.

The town of Hanover, about 30 miles from Apple River Canyon, has the **Whistling Wings Duck Hatchery,** which raises more than 200,000 mallards every year. This is the world center for mallard duck production. The hatchery is on Route 84, in the middle of town. Take home either the fresh or smoked variety for dinner in a handy shipping container; (815) 591–3512.

In October the town holds an **Oktober Duck Festival.** The festival is the first weekend in October and is similar to an old-fashioned Oktoberfest. Write to the Hanover Chamber of Commerce, P.O. Box 537, Hanover 61041, or call (815) 591–2201.

Mount Carroll is pure nineteenth-century Midwest America with its cobblestone courthouse square in the center of town, Victorian architecture, and 1870s-style storefronts lining Main Street. In fact, Mount Carroll was chosen from among seventy-six other Illinois towns as a "Main Street, Illinois" town based on the concept of "building on yesterday for tomorrow."

Mount Carroll, located in the northwest corner of the state, about 10 miles east of the Mississippi River, was named after Charles Carroll, a Maryland signer of the Declaration of Independence. The town was created by an Act of Legislature in 1839.

Appreciative of its architectural treasures, Mount Carroll has preserved many of its original buildings, and a major portion of them are listed in the National Register of Historic Places. A self-guided walking tour through the historical sites is available from the Chamber of Commerce, P.O. Box 94, Mount Carroll 61053.

Highlights of the tour include the **Glenview Hotel,** 116 E. Market Street, built in 1886 at a cost of $20,000. The hotel remained open until 1976. The lobby is decorated with some of the original furniture and a large collection of antiques. The hotel is now an apartment building.

The **Owen P. Miles Home,** located at 107 W. Broadway, has been turned into a museum. It is open Monday through Friday, 10:00 A.M. to 2:00 P.M., Saturday 10:00 A.M. to 3:00 P.M., and Sunday 12:00 to 3:00 P.M., or call (815) 244–3474 for an appointment. It is also open weekdays throughout the year when the curator is in the office.

The Main and Market Streets ✦ **Commercial Core** architecturally dates back to the 1850s, and a number of buildings were faced with galvanized sheet metal. These decorative facades are said to make up one of the finest collections in the United States.

Inside City Hall, 302 N. Main, the United States Hissen brass bell, on loan from the Washington, D.C., Naval Historic Center, is on display.

In the center of the town square is the **War Memorial and**

33

Annex, which is listed in *Ripley's Believe It or Not* as the only memorial with an annex. The annex is to accommodate the 1,284 names listed on the monument. The monument is crowned with a cavalryman designed and sculpted by Lorado Taft, a renowned Midwestern sculptor, lecturer, and author.

Mount Carroll holds an annual **Mayfest,** an arts festival and preservation fair, every Memorial Day weekend. Traditional artisans display their wares, showing examples of smithing, glass, pottery, and performing arts. For a program guide write Mayfest, P.O. Box 94, Mount Carroll 61053; or call (815) 244–9161.

The **Raven's Grin Inn,** at 411 N. Carroll Street (815) 244–4746, is an out-of-body experience for those interested in local artist Jim Warfield's funhouse. Every room is packed with sensory and intellectual experiences. Warfield personally conducts the tours, and no two tours are quite the same.

The Campbell Center is a complex of Georgian Revival buildings previously occupied by Frances Shirmer College. The college was established at Mount Carroll in 1853 and closed in 1978. The center was purchased by the Restoration College Association after Shirmer College closed, and the campus now houses the ✤ **Campbell Center for Historic Preservation.** The center offers workshops in architectural and fine arts preservation, archaeology, and the educational, policy, and planning aspects of preservation. To contact the Campbell Center, call (815) 244–1173 or write Campbell Center for Historic Preservation, S. College Street, Mount Carroll 61053.

The **Oakville County School Museum Complex,** 4 miles southeast of Mount Carroll, is also nostalgic of the nineteenth-century Midwest. A one-room country schoolhouse, a blacksmith shop, and two log cabins are on exhibition. The Carroll County Historical Society operates the complex, and it is open Sunday 2:00 to 4:00 P.M. June 1 through Labor Day and by appointment. Contact the Mount Carroll Chamber of Commerce, P.O. Box 94, Mount Carroll 61053; (815) 244–9161.

Four miles east of Mount Carroll is the **Timber Lake Playhouse,** a live, semiprofessional summer stock theater. The sea-son runs from June 1 to Labor Day, and there are evening and matinee performances. New productions are offered every two weeks along with special children's shows. The 425-seat theater is air-conditioned. For information and tickets write Timber Lake Playhouse, P.O. Box 29, Mount Carroll 61053, or phone (815) 244–2035. Tickets should

Mount Carroll War Memorial

be purchased in advance. For overnight accommodations contact the Mount Carroll Chamber of Commerce; (815) 244–9161.

Farther south along the banks of the Mississippi River is Thomson, home of **Melon Days,** a yearly festival held on Labor Day in which watermelon is the star attraction. Thomson has recently restored its **Burlington Railroad Depot** and turned it into a museum, which is open to the public. For information on festival dates and accommodations, contact Thomson Chamber of Commerce (815) 259–2155.

◆ **Mississippi Palisades State Park** heads up the natural beauty in Carroll County. The 2,550-acre park is located 4 miles north of Savanna and is registered as a national landmark by the Department of the Interior. Its location near the confluence of the Apple and the Mississippi Rivers gives a breathtaking resemblance to tree-lined bluffs along the Hudson River in New York, thus the name palisades. Unusual rock formations have been sculpted by water and wind along the cliffs; among them is Indian Head and the Twin Sisters. There are 12 miles of heavily wooded trails for hiking (the back trails giving the best view of the Mississippi), 5 miles of snowmobile trails, and one hundred acres of open snow area. There are also facilities for picnicking, boating, and camping; a playground; and nature and equestrian trails. For information contact Mississippi Palisades State Park, 4577 U.S. Highway 84 North, Savanna 61074; (815) 273–2731. Hours are from sunup to sundown for the park and 7:30 A.M. to midnight for the campground.

In Lanark the **Standish House,** built in 1882, has been renovated into a bed-and-breakfast. The rooms are furnished with eighteenth- and nineteenth-century English antiques and reproductions. Contact the Standish House at (815) 493–2307 or 540 W. Carroll Street, Lanark 61046.

William "Tutty" Baker, one of the early settlers in Freeport, is responsible for naming the town. Actually it was his wife who teased him about running a "free port" for everyone coming along the trail. Legend has it that one night a group of settlers were discussing a name for the town and Mrs. Baker suggested Freeport because of her husband's generosity.

Freeport is the site of the second Lincoln-Douglas debate, which is marked by a boulder at N. State Avenue and East Douglas Street. The plaque is inscribed with words from both debaters: Lincoln's "This government cannot endure permanently half slave and half free," and Douglas's "I am not for the dissolution of the Union under any circumstances."

The county courthouse, at the junction of U.S. Highway 20 and Route 75, has a ❖ **Civil War Monument,** which was erected in 1869. On the four corners are life-size figures of a Civil War sailor, militiaman, cavalryman, and artilleryman. Engraved on the sides are the names of battles in which Stephenson County volunteers fought. Near the entrance of the courthouse is a plaque commemorating Col. Benjamin Stephenson, Illinois militiaman of 1812.

A bronze statue of Lincoln stands near the entrance to **Taylor's Park,** a mile east of the courthouse on Route 75. **Quality Gardens,** 871 W. Stephenson Street, blooms in the latter part of May and early June and is worth a view.

The **Stephenson County Historical Museum** features memorabilia of early social worker Jane Addams, nineteenth-century furnishings, and an 1840s log cabin. Part of the museum is a farm exhibit, which displays a typical farm kitchen, a blacksmith shop, and many farm machines and tools. A one-room schoolhouse with furnishings dates from approximately 1910.

The museum is located at 1440 S. Carroll Avenue, 4 blocks south of U.S. Highway 20 on Carroll Avenue between Jefferson and Pershing Streets. Admission is free; hours are Wednesday through Sunday noon to 4:00 P.M.; (815) 232–8419. Closed on holidays.

The ❖ **Freeport Art Museum/Arts Council,** at 121 N. Harlem Avenue, has a collection of primitive, Oriental, and American Indian art, European paintings and sculpture, old and new world antiques, plus a contemporary exhibit. It is open Tuesday through Sunday noon to 5:00 P.M., closed holidays. For exhibit information call (815) 235–9755.

Krape Park on Park Boulevard in Freeport is open year-round and has a merry-go-round, flower garden, duck pond, bandshell, boat rentals, tennis courts, miniature golf, and concessions. Open daily; admission is free. Call (815) 235–6114.

Lake Le-Aqua-Na State Park, 6 miles south of the Illinois-Wisconsin state line and 3 miles north of Lena off Route 73, got its name for the nearby town of Lena and *aqua,* the Latin word for water. Roadcuts near the park entrance and to the north contain excellent examples of glacial till with varieties of igneous rock foreign to Illinois. Hours are 6:00 A.M. to sunset from March

16 to November 14, and 8:00 A.M. to sunset from November 15 to March 15; (815) 396–4282. Camping, picnicking, fishing, boating, hiking, and winter sports are available.

The Second Battle of Black Hawk was fought near Kent, and a monument in Kent commemorates the event. The monument is listed in the National Register of Historic Places, and every year the town remembers the battle with a celebration. For information contact the County Clerk's Office, 15 N. Galena Avenue, Freeport 61032; (815) 235–8289.

RONALD REAGAN TERRITORY

Dixon has gained new stature on the Illinois map as the ✦ **President Ronald Reagan Boyhood Home.** Reagan lived at 816 S. Hennepin Avenue from 1920 to 1923, from his ninth to twelfth year. Dixonites consider these his formative years. This house is the only family home in Dixon mentioned in Reagan's autobiography. For hours call (815) 288–3404.

After the Republican National Convention in the summer of 1980, a local mailman noticed that the house was for sale. To preserve the house for future generations, he put down a $250 deposit and raised the remainder of the down payment through donations. A group of local businessmen signed a note to guarantee the mortgage. The house was purchased for $31,500. Fundraising activities and donations paid off the balance of the mortgage by the winter of 1981.

The house and adjacent barn are restored to their 1920 condition; although the furnishings are not those of the Reagan family, they are typical of the time period. The refurbishing was completed in time for Reagan's birthday visit on February 6, 1984.

Listed in the National Register of Historic Places, the home is open to the public free of charge. Volunteers act as interpreters and tour guides. Hours are Monday, Thursday, Friday, and Saturday 10:00 A.M. to 4:00 P.M., Sunday 1:00 to 4:00 p.m; (815) 288–3404.

Dixon is the petunia capital of the world, and to celebrate the city holds a **Petunia Festival** every Fourth of July weekend. The city boasts that more than $7^1/_2$ miles of city streets are lined with petunias. The festival also includes a carnival, games, races, performances at the Dixon Theater, an arts and crafts show, parade, and fireworks. For more information and schedule of events, contact the Chamber of Commerce, 74 Galena Avenue,

Dixon 61021; (815) 284–3361.

Dixon is rich in history as its many monuments to nineteenth-century pioneers testify. On the west bank of the Rock River is the site of ❖ **Fort Dixon,** built during the Black Hawk Wars. On May 13, 1832, a 23-year-old volunteer marched here from Sangamon County. That volunteer was Abraham Lincoln. The **Lincoln Statue,** a statue of Captain Abraham Lincoln when he served in the Black Hawk War of 1832, and the **Old Settler's Memorial Log Cabin** are located on Lincoln Statue Drive on the north bank of the Rock River between Abraham Lincoln Bridge and Ronald Reagan Bridge. The cabin is open only during the summer months.

A nearby granite boulder summarizes Lincoln's military service in the summer of 1832 on a bronze tablet in bas-relief. Another bas-relief shows founding father John Dixon with a picture of Fort Dixon and Dixon's ferry and tavern.

The **Nachusa Hotel,** 215 S. Galena Avenue, is the hotel of the presidents. Five United States presidents have stayed there: Abraham Lincoln, Ulysses S. Grant, Theodore Roosevelt, William Howard Taft, and Ronald Reagan. The hotel was built in 1837 and is the oldest hotel in Illinois. The hotel also claims to have had the first bathtub in Illinois. It is refurbished, and the Abraham Lincoln Room is decorated in authentic 1840 decor. The hotel is no longer operating and is not open to the public, but it's worth driving by.

Nachusa Grasslands on Lowden Road just east of Grand Detour is a privately held nature preserve comprised of sandstone buttes, rolling hills, oak savannahs, wetlands, and a sea of little bluestem grass. For information call (815) 456–2340.

Loveland Community House and Museum, 513 W. Second Street, (815) 284–2741, exhibits local history. Pictures and personal items of John Dixon, a pioneer home, Indian artifacts, and a library with county books and records are part of the exhibit. There is also a Reagan memorabilia section. The curator, a classmate of the former president, has yearbooks and other souvenirs on display and some personal memories to share. Museum hours are Wednesday, Thursday, and Friday 9:00 A.M. to noon, and the first Saturday of the month 9:00 A.M. to 3:00 P.M.

Lowell Park, 3 miles north of Dixon, is a 205-acre park on the Rock River. Ronald Reagan served as a lifeguard here for seven years from 1926 to 1932. On display at **Loveland Community**

Museum is a plaque, which at the time was affixed to a log on the beach. Reagan notched the log every time he saved a life.

The ❖ **Amboy Depot Museum** in Amboy was once the Illinois Central Railroad depot. The 106-year-old building is now a seventeen-room museum telling the history of Amboy. Museum hours are weekends and holidays only from 1:00 to 4:00 P.M, May 1 through November 1. Admission is free. No phone, but Amboy is a small community and the museum is easy to find on East Avenue.

Two memorials are near the Amboy depot. One is on the original site of the Carson Pirie Scott & Company department store, the other is a memorial to the early history of the Reorganized Church of Latter Day Saints.

Grand Detour is an unincorporated area with about 400 inhabitants, but thousands of tourists visit each year because of a blacksmith named John Deere who opened a shop there in 1836. The shop was the beginning of Deere and Company, one of the largest manufacturers of plows in the world.

Grand Detour was named by the Indians because of the oxbow bend in the Rock River at this point. In 1834, pioneer Leonard Andres came to the Rock River Valley and made a claim to the land. He laid out the village of Grand Detour, but, unfortunately, the town was passed over by the railroad and never grew to its early promise of prosperity.

When Deere started farming here, he found that plowing the heavy soil was a difficult job and that most settlers gave up in despair. He experimented with different shapes and materials for plows, and in 1837 he developed a steel plow that worked. Deere and Company is now the oldest major manufacturing business in Illinois and the largest producer of farm implements in the world.

The John Deere Foundation maintains buildings and features of the original property in Grand Detour. An archaeological exhibition building covers the site of the original blacksmith shop and displays various machines and how they work. The ❖ **John Deere Historic Site** also includes Deere's house, authentically furnished from the 1830s, a visitors center, and a blacksmith shop reconstructed on the basis of archaeological findings. The shop has a working forge and equipment used by nineteenth-century iron craftsmen.

The John Deere Historic Site is open daily 9:00 A.M. to 5:00 P.M., April through October 31. Admission is $3.00 for people ages 16 and older. For further information contact the John Deere Historic Site, R.R. 3, Grand Detour 61021; (815) 652–4551.

Another attraction in Ogle County is the **Ogle County Courthouse** in the center of Oregon. The building is listed in the National Register of Historic Places, and a Soldier's Monument designed by Lorado Taft adorns the lawn.

Lowden State Park, across the river from Oregon, is on a bluff overlooking the Rock River. ◆ **Black Hawk,** Lorado Taft's most famous statue, stands 50 feet high overlooking the area. Taft and a few artists retreated to this area every summer during the 1920s and created an artists' colony known as Eagle's Nest. The public library in Oregon has a collection of works by Taft on display in the second-floor gallery.

White Pines State Forest, (815) 946–3717, 8 miles west of Oregon, has 385 acres of recreation and forest area. The lodge has a restaurant, gift shop, and lounge. There are also twenty-six cabins and tent and trailer camping. The park is open from 8:00 A.M. to sundown year-round. For information concerning the lodge

John Deere Historic Site

and restaurant, call (815) 946–3817.

Mount Morris, northwest of Oregon, has the **Freedom Bell** dedicated by Ronald Reagan in 1963. The bell was hung in the Illinois Pavilion in the 1964 World's Fair and again at a 1965 Cubs' game in Wrigley Field. It is a replica of the Liberty Bell in Philadelphia and is the focal point of the **Let Freedom Ring Festival** every Fourth of July in Mount Morris.

Fulton celebrates its Dutch heritage on the first weekend in May every year. **Dutch Days** are highlighted by *klompen* (wooden shoe) dancing in the the streets of the town. A parade is preceded by the *burgemeester* (mayor) and the town crier inspecting the streets to see if they are clean. When the mayor announces that "We must scrub the streets," costumed street cleaners come out with brooms and pails and scrub until the streets are declared clean.

One part of the parade is the "Parade of Provinces," where townspeople wear native costumes from each province of the Netherlands. *Sinterclas*, the Dutch version of Santa Claus, brings up the rear of the parade.

Delft jewelry and dishes, wooden shoes, and authentic costumes are on sale. Local stores offer tastes of Dutch cheese and pastry. Traditional Dutch meals, which include corned beef, potatoes and cabbage, pea soup, and currant buns, are served.

The townspeople plant more than 10,000 tulip bulbs every year, and windmills and tulips are in great profusion in Fulton. Even the information booth is housed in a windmill.

During Dutch Days the town crier walks the street announcing special events, and the library displays Dutch books and shows films of the Netherlands (no admission charged).

The festival ends Sunday afternoon with a traditional Dutch worship at a Fulton church. Men and women sit on opposite sides of the church, and part of the service is conducted in Dutch.

For information contact Fulton Chamber of Commerce, P.O. Box 253, Fulton 61252; (815) 589–4545.

Prophetstown State Park, in Prophetstown, was once the site of the Winnebago Indian tribal village. The park derives its name from the Indian prophet Wa-bo-kie-shiek (White Cloud). The village was destroyed in the Black Hawk Indian War of 1832. The park borders the Rock River on the northeast side of Prophetstown. Picnicking, fishing, and camping are available, but with no lifeguards here, plan on swimming at the city park, just 4 blocks away. Call (815) 537–2926 for more information about Prophetstown State Park.

Sterling is the location of the **P.W. Dillon Home Museum.** The Italian Renaissance-style brick home at 1005 E. Third Street was built on the five-and-one-half-acre lot in 1857. Paul W. Dillon, owner of Northwestern Steel and Wire Company, lived there for ninety-six years from his birth in 1883 until his death in 1980. The home has antiques and artifacts on display, plus an Engine #73 steam locomotive and caboose. Hours are Tuesday, Thursday, and Saturday 10:00 A.M. to noon and 1:00 to 4:00 P.M., and Sunday 1:00 to 5:00 P.M.; (815) 622–6215.

The two **Lincoln historical markers** in Sterling are at 607 E. Third Street and at Sixth Avenue and Sixth Street. A **founder's historical plaque** is at Fourth Street and Broadway, the **Grandon Civic Center** is at Third Avenue, and a **Civil War Monument and bandshell** are at E. Fourth Street.

Morrison-Rockwood State Park on Route 78 is located 2½ miles north of Morrison. Lake Carlton, at the center of the park, has a 38-foot-high, 1,800-foot-long dam with a road across it. Fishing, boating, camping, picnicking, and hiking are available. Call (815) 772–4708.

The **Old Grist Mill** in Morrison is no longer open to the public but can be seen from U.S. Highway 30 on the west side of Morrison.

Union Grove Cemetery, also on U.S. Highway 30 just outside Morrison, dates back to the early 1800s and is open to the public.

Route 84, running along the west edge of Whiteside County, is part of the **Great River Road** that parallels the Mississippi River and is one of the most scenic drives in Illinois.

Time doesn't stand still in Rockford. The ◆ **Time Museum,** 7801 E. State Street, (815) 398–6000, illustrates the historical development of timekeeping devices from 3000 B.C. to the present. The museum covers the evolution of time measurement from Stonehenge to the atomic clock, and its world-famous collection spans 5,000 years. The many different kinds of clocks and watches—a total of 3,000 pieces—on display include sundials, astrolabes, nocturnals, compendiums, incense timekeepers, water clocks, sandglasses, calendars, chronometers, and navigational instruments.

The Time Museum Bookshop has publications on time measurement as well as a variety of art books, children's books, jewelry, and souvenirs. Museum hours are Tuesday through Saturday

10:00 A.M. to 5:00 P.M. Admission is $3.00 for adults, $2.00 for senior citizens, and $1.00 for children under 12.

Rockford has many museums for those who love browsing. The **Midway Village and Museum Center,** 6799 Guilford Road, (815) 397–9112, has a history building featuring local history, an industrial building with thirty-two local industries represented, and Midway Village, a turn-of-the-century village complete with stagecoaches. The village has law offices, a blacksmith shop, an old stone school, a town hall, lumber shops, a jail, a sheriff's office, and a bandstand. Admission fees are $3.00 for adults, $2.00 for senior citizens, and $1.00 for children under 12. The center is open Monday through Friday 10:00 A.M. to 4:00 P.M., noon to 4:00 P.M. Saturday and Sunday.

The ❖ **Burpee Museum of Natural History,** 813 Main Street, (815) 965–3132, and the **Burpee Art Museum,** 737 N. Main Street, (815) 965–3131, are both housed in Victorian mansions. They are open Thursday through Saturday afternoons.

The **Discovery Center,** 711 S. Main Street, (815) 963–6769, is a "hands-on" participatory museum where you can explore scientific and perceptual principles. The center is open Tuesday through Sunday 1:00 to 4:00 P.M. Summer hours are daily 1:00 to 4:00 P.M.

The **Erlander Home Museum,** operated by the Swedish Historical Society, has mementoes of Rockford's rich Swedish history. It is located at 404 S. Third Street, (815) 963–5559. Hours are Sunday 2:00 to 4:00 P.M.

The **Graham-Ginestra House,** 1115 S. Main Street, (815) 968–6044, is an example of classic Greek Revival and Italianate architecture. It has elaborately painted ceilings and authentic furnishings. It is open 2:00 to 4:00 P.M. the first Sunday of each month and is listed in the National Register of Historic Places.

Victorian Village, Longwood Avenue, offers twenty shops containing antiques and artwork. You'll find a restaurant, a needlework shop, and a tea room. The village is just off Business Highway 20 between Sixth and Ninth Streets.

❖ **Tinker Swiss Cottage** was built in the Swiss-chalet style after its owner, Robert Hall Tinker, visited Switzerland in 1862. The cottage's antique treasures include a 300-year-old painting, diamond-dust mirrors, Lincoln memorabilia, and dozens of family heirlooms. The cottage is open Wednesday through Sunday, with tours at 1:00 p.m. and 3:00 P.M. Call (815) 964–2424 or write 411 Kent Street, Rockford 61102.

◆ **Magic Waters,** a wave pool, offers a children's playground beach, a 40-inch-wide roller slide, and organized games, activities (including aerobics classes), and competitions. Magic Waters is located just off I–90 at the U.S. Highway 20/U.S. Highway 51 interchange near Rockford. Call (815) 332–3280 or write Magic Waters, 7820 CherryVale North Boulevard, Cherry Valley 61016.

◆ **Rock Cut State Park,** off Route 173 about 6 miles northeast of Rockford, has picnicking, camping, trails, fishing, boating, ice skating, ice fishing, cross-country skiing, and snowmobiling. From Rockford take U.S. Highway 51 to Route 173. For information contact the Site Superintendent, 7318 Harlem Road, Caledonia 61011; (815) 885–3311.

One of the best ways to see this area is to follow the carefully mapped Boone County Historical Trail. Originally compiled by the Boone County Bicentennial Commission and the Boone County Conservation District in 1976, the guide to the trail is available by calling (815) 547–7935.

The trail follows four different routes: the South Pacific Route, running through a region once covered by more than 50 miles of native prairie grasslands; Belvidere/Caledonia Route, covering the county seat, Belvidere, and the Scottish settlements at Caledonia and Argyle; Piscasaw Route, which follows the Kishwaukee River and Piscasaw Creek to the Norwegian village of Capron; and the Blaine/State Line Route, beginning in the Kinnikinnick Creek Conservation Acre and traveling through historic Blaine village and across the rolling hills of the Illinois-Wisconsin border. Each route is about 30 miles long, approximating the length of one day's wagon trip in the early settlement days of the 1830s. The trail is designed to be covered by car, on foot by hikers, or on bicycles.

The first three routes begin in Belvidere's Spencer Park, on the western edge of the city on Lincoln Avenue. Before the arrival of white settlers, this was the permanent gathering place for the local Potawatomi Indians. At nearby Belvidere Park, the old **Baltic Mill** dates from 1845 and was in use up until 1918. The fall of water through the Kishwaukee River provided the basic energy to turn the heavy grinding wheel.

At 534 E. Hurlbut Avenue is the former home of one of its early Civil War heroes, Gen. Stephen A. Hurlbut. Hurlbut's forces at the Battle of Shiloh won an important victory for the Union, earning him national recognition. He served as a member of the Illinois Constitutional Convention, a state representative in the

45

Illinois Legislature, a U.S. congressman, and a minister to Colombia and Peru. Hurlbut is buried in Belvidere Cemetery along with dozens of the city's pioneers.

Usually cemeteries are repositories of an area's history, and Belvidere Cemetery, at N. Main and Harrison Streets, is no exception. Stop at the cemetery office, (815) 547–7642, for a copy of their historic walking tour. Established in 1847, the burial ground holds the graves of two Revolutionary War soldiers, Thomas Hart and Timothy Lewis; the first white woman in the county, Sara Loop; a black soldier in the Civil War and former slave, John Lawson; and blacksmith Samuel Longcor. Longcor was an early Illinois manufacturer of scouring plows, known as the S. Longcor's Iron Beam, a significant development in the cultivation of the state's prairie lands.

The **Pettit Memorial Chapel,** listed in the National Register of Historic Places, was designed by Frank Lloyd Wright in 1907 as a monument to a local physician, Dr. William H. Pettit. The chapel was restored by the Belvidere Junior Women's Club in 1977. It is a fine example of Wright's Prairie School style, with long, low lines. The stucco exterior is painted pale green with dark green wood trim and has a rough sawn cedar shingle roof. Contact the cemetery office (number above) for viewing or a list of open dates.

Another historic home, the **Colonel Joel Walker Home**, stands at the corner of Lincoln Avenue and Main Street. The 1840 structure was the residence of a noted hero of the War of 1812.

Big Thunder Park honors the Potawatomi Indian Chief Big Thunder, who died before the first white settlers arrived on the scene in the 1830s. His method of burial, however, provided the town's very first tourist attraction. Following Indian custom, he was buried seated in his best attire, along with food, tobacco, and implements necessary in the afterlife, then surrounded by a 6-foot-tall log stockade and left to the elements. Early visitors, including travelers on the Chicago-Galena stagecoach who stopped here, were very curious and—like tourists today—took souvenirs. Soon, very little was left of Big Thunder. But undaunted, the local citizenry substituted bones of hogs and sheep, it is said, as relics for the eager and gullible tourists. A boulder with bronze plaque on the grounds of the Boone County courthouse serves as a memorial.

A greater exploration of local history can be undertaken at the **Boone County Historical Museum,** 311 Whitney Boulevard;

(815) 544–8391. Featured are farm implements typical of those that shaped the county's character. Call for appointments.

The area's major employer is the Chrysler Belvidere Plant, at 3000 W. Chrysler Drive off U.S. 20 Bypass. Its 3,500 employees turn out Chrysler and Dodge's most popular cars. During some parts of the year, plant tours can be arranged by appointment on Fridays only. Call (815) 547–2109.

The fall in Belvidere is the time for festivals. The third weekend in September brings **Oktoberfest** to town, with German bands, beer, and food, along with carnival rides and craft exhibits. The fourth weekend in September each year, the Boone County Conservation District sponsors the **Autumn Pioneer Festival** with pioneer ethnic gardens, produce, samples and crafts, volunteers in authentic period dress, and an Indian village. Call (815) 547–7935.

Northwest of Belvidere are remnants of the county's immigrant past when Scottish and Scandinavian settlers arrived to take up farming. **Caledonia** and **Argyle** (on the Winnebago County line) were, of course, Scottish settlements. In 1834 two Armour brothers and their cousin came to Ottawa, Illinois, from Kintyre, Scotland. Shortly thereafter they moved to this part of Boone County, which came to be known as Scotch Grove.

Capron, on Route 173 in the northeast part of the county, was home to Norwegian settlers. The first two Norwegian pioneers came to the area in 1842 and called their settlement Helgesaw, later known as Long Prairie.

The town of DeKalb can, quite legitimately, claim that it changed the future of the American West. Once known as the "World's Barbed Wire Capital," it was here in 1874 that inventor Joseph F. Glidden patented an improved method of producing barbed wire. An industry grew up around his invention, with other DeKalb pioneers involved in its manufacture—Jacob Haish and Isaac Ellwood. The **Glidden homestead** and barn at 921 West Lincoln Highway is listed in the National Register of Historic Places. It's privately owned, however, and not open to the public.

The **Ellwood House Museum,** 509 N. First Street, is an imposing Victorian mansion appointed with the finest furnishings of the period. Call (815) 756–4609 for hours. Also in Ellwood Park is the Little House, a 10-foot miniature mansion with carefully crafted interiors. The carriage house on the property has a fine collection of buggies and sleighs and samples of—what else?—barbed wire. Admission is $4.00 adults; under 12, free.

Northern Illinois University, founded in 1895, is located in DeKalb. The school, with 25,000 enrollment, is the second largest in the state. The architecture of some of the older buildings is worth exploring. Check with the Office of Admissions in Williston Hall for guided tours of the campus and self-guided walking tours; (815) 753–0446. NIU's O'Connell and Players' Theaters offer performances throughout the year; (815) 753–1600. Admission is free to the anthropology museum in the Stevens Building.

The **Egyptian Theater,** on North Second Street near Lincoln Highway, is a National Register of Historic Places building with a unique terra-cotta exterior and excellent acoustics. Built in the Egyptian Revival style, the theater is used for productions by traveling companies and local performing arts groups, as well as for movies; (815) 758–1215. Tours are scheduled by appointment only for $2.00 per person.

The 1929 **Haish Memorial Library,** at Oak and N. Third Streets, was a gift from another early barbed wire baron. Its art deco Indiana limestone structure, designed by White and Weber of Chicago, was also placed in the National Register.

The **Gurler House,** 205 Pine Street, is home to a series of special events, such as the Summers Eve Festival. The Greek Revival farmhouse, set in a parklike environment, is listed in the National Register. Historically speaking, DeKalb also claims the first county farm bureau—in 1912.

Festivals of all kinds are important in the county. Among the most popular is the annual **Sweet Corn Festival** each August in DeKalb (with free corn on the cob); Sycamore, the county seat, hosts a yearly **Pumpkin Festival** the last weekend in October with a variety of old-time activities including a parade and decorated pumpkins on the courthouse lawn; (815) 895–3456.

Shabbona Lake State Park, in the southwest part of DeKalb County, encompasses 1,550 acres and a 32-acre lake. Fishing is the thing here, and boats can be rented ($40/day for motorboats, $20/day for rowboats) at the marina. One hundred-fifty campsites are available (all with electrical hookups), and hiking trails, horseshoe pits, and a baseball diamond are in place. In the winter, cross-country skiing, ice fishing, and snowmobiling are enjoyed here. Write the Site Superintendent, RR 1, Box 120, Shabbona 60550; (815) 824–2106.

In the southeast corner of the county, Sandwich is home of the popular **Sandwich Antiques Market,** May to October from 8:00 A.M. to 4:00 P.M. Sundays at the County Fairgrounds on U.S. Highway 34. Admission is $4.00; parking is free.

INDIANS AND SOLDIERS

Ottawa is a town that remembers its soldiers well. **Washington Park,** in the center of town, between Lafayette and La Salle Streets, has two war memorials, one dedicated to veterans of World Wars I and II, Vietnam, and Korea, and the other to the county soldiers in the Civil War. The Civil War monument was designed and erected by Edward McInhill, and it lists the names of the soldiers.

The park is a block square and is decorated with flowers and shrubbery. During the summer months an old-fashioned popcorn wagon does business, and piped music plays in the park. Many of the townspeople enjoy their lunch there.

The park also has a boulder for commemorating the first Lincoln-Douglas debate here on August 21, 1858. The memorial was erected by the Illinois Chapter of the Daughters of the American Revolution.

In 1856 Sheriff William Reddick built what is known as the ◆ **Reddick Mansion.** The building is at 100 W. Lafayette Street, across the street from Washington Park and is listed as a national landmark. It serves as office space for the Ottawa Chamber of Commerce and as a tourist information center.

The **Third District Appellate Court of Illinois,** just east of the Reddick Mansion, was built in 1857 and served as the state's supreme court for a decade. The building is open to visitors during business hours.

Other attractions to see in Ottawa include the **statue of W. D. Boyce,** who founded the Boy Scouts of America in 1910. The statue is in the Ottawa Avenue Cemetery, 1 mile west of downtown Ottawa on Boyce Memorial Drive. Boyce is buried near the statue.

Christ Episcopal Church was the first Episcopal church to hold services in Ottawa in 1838. It is an example of English High Victorian Gothic architecture. The Wallace Window, patterned after a cathedral in Glasgow, Scotland, is a depiction of the Resurrection. It was designed by Professor Julius Herber of Dresden, Germany, one of Germany's finest artists. The church is located at 113 W. Lafayette Street.

The Ottawa Silica Company office, an example of classic Geor-

49

gian architecture, is west of downtown on Boyce Memorial Drive.

The old **4978 Locomotive and weight car** was donated to Ottawa by the Chicago, Burlington, and Quincy Railroad in 1966. It is next to the Silica Company office.

The **Ottawa Avenue Memorial Columns** are classic Roman architecture. The columns were built in 1918 as a memorial to Ottawa in honor of the centennial celebration of Illinois statehood. The columns are located next to the Ottawa Avenue Cemetery. Allen Park, along the Illinois River where it joins the Fox River, is a scenic park with tennis courts, public boat launches, picnic areas, and a beautiful view of the two rivers.

The Ottawa Chamber of Commerce publishes an auto tour of historic sites in the city. Contact the chamber for a copy of the tour at Ottawa Chamber of Commerce, 100 W. Lafayette Street, P.O. Box 888, Ottawa 61350, (815) 433–0084, or call the Heritage Corridor Visitors Bureau at (815) 433–1355.

Two miles west of Ottawa in the Illinois Michigan Canal National Heritage Corridor is the ◆ **Effigy Tumuli.** These five massive earth sculptures have been shaped into a mile-and-a-half-long work, the largest outdoor sculpture in the world. Call (815) 942–0796 for information.

The **Starved Rock Land Tour,** also available at the Chamber of Commerce office, begins just outside the Ottawa Avenue Cemetery in the village of Naplate. The village was named for the former National Plate Glass Company and is now the home of the Libbey-Owens-Ford Glass Company.

The tour continues west through **Buffalo Rock State Park,** named for the rock that resembles a sleeping bison, to the Half-Way House, once the Sulphur Springs Hotel. The house is privately owned and not open to the public.

The **Grand Village of the Kaskaskia Indians** (1678 to 1700) is the site of three archaeological excavations near the Illinois River. Artifacts from the digs are on exhibit at the La Salle County Historical Museum in Utica.

The **Starved Rock Lock and Dam** and **Illinois Waterway Visitors Center** are next on the tour, followed by the **Father Marquette Memorial.**

The **La Salle County Historical Museum** in Utica, just outside Starved Rock State Park, was built during the term of President Zachary Taylor in 1848.

The tour ends at the Visitors Center in ◆ **Starved Rock**

State Park. Starved Rock State Park is located 10 miles west of Ottawa on Route 71 or south of I–80 on Route 178.

The park's name was derived from an Indian legend, which originated during the 1760s when Pontiac, chief of the Ottawa tribe (which lived upriver from this area), was murdered by an Illinois Indian while attending a tribal council in southern Illinois. Many battles to avenge the death of Pontiac were fought, and the Potawatomi tribe, allies of the Ottawa, fought the Illinois Indians in the area called Starved Rock. The Illinois Indians took refuge on top of a butte and were surrounded by the Ottawa and Potawatomi tribes. They eventually starved atop the rock.

There is evidence the Archaic Indians as well as the Hopewellian, Woodland, and Mississippian tribes lived in the area. Village sites and burial mounds have been mapped by archaeologists within the park boundaries.

The largest group of Indians to inhabit the area was the Illinois. They are believed to have lived here from the 1500s to the 1700s. The tribe's population was between 5,000 and 10,000 and was divided into subtribes. The Kaskaskias were a subtribe whose village extended along the north bank of the Illinois River, directly across from the park.

French explorers Louis Joliet and Father Jacques Marquette were the first known Europeans to visit the area. They canoed up the Illinois River from the Mississippi and stopped at the Kaskaskia village. Two years later, Father Marquette founded the Mission of Immaculate Conception, Illinois's first Christian mission, on the site of the Kaskaskia village.

Rene Robert Cavalier, Sieur de La Salle, came to the area to build a chain of forts to confine the English colonies in the East. Fort St. Louis was built on top of Starved Rock in the winter of 1682–83. It was a strategic post, towering above the rapids of the Illinois River and thereby controlling passage from Canada south. Many Indians settled near the fort for protection from the Iroquois tribe and to be near French trade goods.

In the 1800s there was a movement to make Starved Rock the "Gibraltar of the West," but this plan was unsuccessful. The area was later developed into a vacation spot. In 1911 the State of Illinois purchased Starved Rock and the surrounding area. The park now consists of 2,630 acres and is bordered by a 582–acre nature preserve.

Many interesting rock formations are found in the park; they are primarily of St. Peter's sandstone, laid down by a huge, shallow inland sea more than 425 million years ago. It was brought to the surface by an enormous upfold known as the La Salle Anticline. Continual erosion has formed the existing flat surface.

Most of the flat land was glaciated during the past 700,000 years, resulting in a flat and gently rolling plain formed after the last glacier. Most of the prairie is now farmland, and the areas along the river are predominantly forest.

There are eighteen canyons in the park; they were formed by streams feeding into the Illinois River. The streams cut channels through the rock as they followed the cracks and crevices of the sedimentary layers. Waterfalls are found at the heads of all the canyons, especially after a hard summer rain. The most popular waterfalls are at the St. Louis, French, La Salle, and Ottawa canyons.

The park has a wide variety of plant and animal life. Red oak, basswood, and sugar maple trees grow in the moist, sandy soil along the northern slopes. Woodchucks feed on the lush undergrowth, and moles live on insects found in the soil. Vireos and catbirds fly above the ferns and shrubs. Trillium, Dutchmen's Breeches, and the large white flowers of the May Apple tree can be seen in spring.

Along the floodplain cottonwood, black willow, and ash trees grow. Skunk cabbage, marsh marigold, and wild iris live in the marshy areas. Wood ducks nest in hollow trees and can be seen paddling along the river's edge. Beaver and muskrat sometimes appear along the river.

The park has 20 miles of marked hiking trails, and hiking information is available at the visitors center and park office. The trails are open year-round, but hikers should be cautious near bluffs and stay on official park trails. Metal trail maps are located at all trail access points, trail intersections, and points of interest. Colored dots along the trails and on trees assist the hiker; the correspond to letter symbols on trail maps.

Picnicking is permitted, and picnic tables, drinking water, toilets, litter cans, and metal grills are provided at no charge.

Fishing is permitted but anglers must stay 600 feet from the dam. Channel catfish are caught between the lock and dam, bullheads from the seawall, white bass from both ends of Plum Island, sauger and walleye from below the dam in fast water, carp from both banks, and crappies from around the small Leopold Island.

Boats may be launched from the ramp at the west end of the park, and canoes are available for rent.

Ice skating is permitted at parking lot C, and cross-country skiing and snowshoeing are allowed in the picnic area and at **Mattiessen State Park** (just southeast of Starved Rock State Park off Route 178). Equipment can be rented on weekends, and tobogganing and sledding are permitted east of parking lot C. Heated washrooms are accessible from these areas. Snowmobiling is not allowed in the park.

The visitors center displays the park's cultural and natural history. A park interpreter posts a weekly schedule of activities. The center is usually open on weekend afternoons during peak visitor seasons. If the center is closed, contact the park office, which is open daily from 8:00 A.M. to 4:00 P.M.

Contact the visitors center or park interpreter at Starved Rock State Park, Box 116, Utica 61373; (815) 667–4906.

Camping is permitted except in the winter and during the spring thaw. There are 133 sites, and permits are obtained at the campground or park office.

There are horseback riding trails and a horseback riders' campground along Route 71 in the far western side of the park. Horse rentals are available on weekends on Route 71, half a mile west of Route 178.

The **Starved Rock Lodge,** inside the state park, is located on a high bluff overlooking the Illinois River. It has seventy-two rooms and a rustic lounge with a large double fireplace. The lobby is available for public and private use. An indoor swimming pool, Jacuzzi, and sauna are also available. The Pow-Wow Room in the lodge basement offers refreshments. Eighteen cabins adjacent to the lodge are also for rent. Lodging is available year-round. For reservations and information call (815) 667–4211 or write Starved Rock Lodge, Schmidt Enterprises, Inc., P.O. Box 471, Utica 61373.

Norway, 12 miles northeast of Ottawa, is the site of the first permanent settlement of Norwegians in 1834. Inspired by their leader, Cleng Peerson, fourteen families purchased a tiny sailing vessel and set sail for America. They left Norway because of economic, political, and religious domination by the Swedes. Peerson became known as the Norwegian Daniel Boone because he helped settle the new land in America.

A historical marker on Route 71 commemorates the hundred-year anniversary of the settlement, and a plaque tells the Norsk story. The **Norsk Museum,** off Route 71 on County Road 2631, is open May through October, Saturday and Sunday from 1:00 to 5:00 P.M.

Great elm trees planted by the founding fathers line the streets of Princeton, a prosperous small town much like it was when it was part of the pioneer path to the west.

Princeton was the home of the abolitionist preacher Owen Lovejoy. Lovejoy, a close friend of Abraham Lincoln, was elected to the State Legislature in 1854 and then to the U.S. House of Representatives in 1856 where he served five terms. Lovejoy became nationally known for his work on behalf of the abolition of slavery. His house was one of the most important stations on the Underground Railway in Illinois. Runaway slaves were hidden here by the Lovejoy family until plans could be made for them to travel to the next station on their way to Canada.

The ♦ **Owen Lovejoy Homestead** is now a museum. Listed in the National Register of Historic Places, it has fifteen rooms and has been restored to reflect the typical furnishing of its era. The home is on U.S. Highway 6 in Princeton. Hours are 1:00 to 5:00 P.M. everyday except Tuesday. For additional information write Tour Director, 451 S. Main Street, Princeton 61356; (815) 875–2184.

More recent history can be found on the shelves of **Hoffman's Patterns of the Past,** a china and crystal replacement service at 513 S. Main Street. More than 12,000 hard-to-find patterns are stocked. Hours are 9:00 A.M. to 5:00 P.M. Monday through Saturday; (815) 875–1944.

Other buildings to look for in Princeton are the **Cyrus Bryant House,** 1110 S. Main Street, and the **John Bryant House** at 1518 S. Main Street. Cyrus Bryant's house was built in 1844, and in the front yard is a boulder marking the site of the log cabin that he and his brother John built when they gained the right to buy public land by settling on it.

Another attraction in Princeton is the red covered bridge built in 1863. The bridge is 2½ miles north of Princeton off Route 26.

The second weekend in September is the **Homestead Festival and Annual Pork Barbeque,** complete with an ice cream social, art show, beer garden, street dance, flea market, antique car show, pioneer crafts, horse-drawn wagons, and horse show. For information contact the Princeton Chamber of Commerce, 435 S. Main Street, Princeton 61356; (815) 875–2616.

Covered Bridge in Princeton

The **Hennepin Canal Parkway State Park,** 1 mile south of I–80 at Route 88, is a 104-mile waterway with canoeing, boating, hiking, and snowmobiling. It was here that engineers discovered how to make water run uphill. The park is open twenty-four hours a day. Call (815) 454–2328.

In 1846 a group of idealistic Swedish immigrants came to the Midwest looking for a place to build a communal society. Under the leadership of Erik Janson, a religious zealot, the group founded a commune in ◆ **Bishop Hill.** The group, industrious and optimistic, suffered through a harsh winter and epidemics. That year took many of its inhabitants with it. The survivors did establish their version of utopia, but dissension spread among the ranks, and in 1861 the commune dissolved. With the dissolution Bishop Hill faded into history.

Almost twenty years ago the descendents of the Jansonists decided to restore Bishop Hill. The town is now listed as a National

Historic Landmark and as a historic district in the National Register of Historic Places. The preserved buildings, located mostly in the center of town, trace the history of the commune.

The **Steeple Building,** once the commune's church, is now a museum. In it craftspeople re-create colony life by demonstrating crafts and other skills practiced by the Jansonists. The museum also has an exhibit of world-famous primitive paintings by Olaf Krans. Admission is $1.00 for adults and 50 cents for children.

The **Colony Church** has also been restored into a museum and has changing exhibits. It is open from 9:00 A.M. to 5:00 P.M., Wednesday through Sunday. The ❖ **Bjorklund Hotel,** now restored, is open for visitors but not overnight guests. Both the Steeple Building and the hotel are open daily from 9:00 A.M. to 5:00 P.M. except holidays.

Bishop Hill has twenty-two gift and craft shops that sell antiques, Swedish imports, and handicrafts. Local restaurants serve Swedish and American food. For information contact the Bishop Hill Heritage Association, P.O. Box 1853, Bishop Hill 61419; (309) 927–3899.

The **Henry County Historical Museum** is also located in Bishop Hill, a block south of the town park. Its thousands of artifacts tell of the county's history. Included in its collection are garments, tools, gadgets, and furnishings of the late nineteenth century. Five display areas are devoted to special interest subjects, and the exhibits are changed during the season. A nineteenth-century bedroom, a harness shop, and a parlor organ are on permanent display. Museum hours are daily from 10:00 A.M. to 4:00 P.M. May through October.

The last weekend in September is the **Jordbruksdagarna**— the harvest fest. For specific dates and a list of activities, call the Bishop Hill Heritage Association at (309) 927–3899.

Overnight accommodations in Bishop Hill are available at the **Holden Guest House;** (309) 927–3500.

Two miles north of Woodhull on County Road 400 at 63E is **Max Nordeen's Wheels Museum,** a personal collection of 2,300 items organized around automotive history. The museum is open June through August daily except Mondays and on weekends only in May, September, and October. Hours are 9:00 A.M. to 4:00 P.M.; (309) 334–2589.

About 6 miles southeast of Bishop Hill on U.S. Route 34 is Galva, the sister city to Gävle, Sweden. Galva is the home of

Jacobsen's Home Bakery, which specializes in rusks, a sweet raised bread toasted until brown and crisp. The rusks are sold in food stores in a 50-mile radius of Galva and are mail ordered around the country.

Jenny Lind, the famous Swedish opera singer, endowed a chapel in Andover, just northwest of Bishop Hill on Route 81. The chapel is open to the public.

The **Henry County Courthouse,** built in 1878–80, is located in Cambridge, the county seat. The main courtroom is worth a look. It is decorated with murals depicting the principal communities in the county.

Henry County has a number of lakes and recreational parks for camping, swimming, fishing, picnicking, hiking, boating, and waterskiing. **Johnson Sauk State Park,** off Route 78, 4 miles south of the Annawan exit of I–80, has 400 acres of campsites along the Old Sauk Trail. **Izaak Walton League Park,** Route 82, 1½ miles north of Genesco on Hennepin Canal Parkway, has eight acres of camping, fishing, hiking, and water sports. The **Circle S Campground** on Route 78 has eighty acres of wooded area and fifty campsites. Circle S is 4 miles north of the Annawan exit on I–80. The **Timber Campground,** 5 miles north of Bishop Hill, has twenty campsites with lake swimming, fishing, a pavilion, and planned activities. It is located on Route 81, 3 miles east of Cambridge and 1 mile north.

Rock Island, one of the Quad Cities, has the Mississippi River as its frontyard and the Rock River as its back. During the 1840s and 1850s, the height of the steamboat era, as many as 1,900 steamboats docked in Rock Island annually.

It was here in 1675 that explorers Marquette and Joliet came on their trip down the Mississippi River. Seven years later they were driven out by the Sauk and Fox tribes. In 1805 Zebulon Pike traveled up the Mississippi on a government inspection trip and found the land inhabited by more than 5,000 Indians.

In 1816 Rock Island was fortified by the government and Col. George Davenport became the first resident-settler. In 1828 other settlers started moving here in large numbers and began battling with the Indians. The Indians retaliated, and the settlers sent for help from the governor. They wrote that the Indians "threaten our lives if we attempt to plant corn, and say that we have stolen their land from them, and they are determined to exterminate us."

The result was the Black Hawk War in which the Sauk and Fox

57

lost their fight, opening up all of northern Illinois for settlement.

The Rock Island Railway, the first to come to the area, completed its railroad bridge in 1855, the first bridge to span the entire Mississippi River.

In 1862 the ✦ **Rock Island Arsenal** was built. It originally served as a prison for Confederate soldiers, and more than 1,200 prisoners were confined here. When the Civil War ended, the arsenal was converted to its present use as the U.S. Army Armament, Munition, and Chemical Command.

The Rock Island Arsenal was built on what is now known as Arsenal Island, in the middle of the Mississippi River. The arsenal is one of the largest in the world.

The **Clock Tower,** the first permanent building of the Rock Island Arsenal, has a giant clock, over a hundred years old and still running. Visitors can tour the Clock Tower (on weekends and by appointment only) and other sights on the island—a replica of the **Fort Armstrong blockhouse,** the **Court of Patriots Memorial,** and a Confederate Soldier Cemetery. For tour information contact the visitors center at Lock and Dam 15 on Arsenal Island.

Lock and Dam 15 Visitors Center stands above the Mississippi Waterway System, where you can get a great view of barges passing through the lock system. Admission is free. The center is open daily in the summer months 9:00 A.M. to 9:00 P.M., spring and fall 9:00 A.M. to 5:00 P.M., winter 9:00 A.M. to 5:00 P.M., closed from December 15 to February 3. Call (309) 788–6412 for information about the above mentioned sites and about the Davenport home.

The restored **home of Colonel Davenport** is open for viewing Saturday and Sunday from 1:00 to 3:00 P.M., from the first weekend in May through October. It is located on Davenport Drive on Arsenal Island (which was called Rock Island when he settled here, before the town of Rock Island grew in size).

For bikers an 8-mile bike trail around Arsenal Island begins at Terrace Drive at the corner of Gillespie Street.

To reach Arsenal Island take I–74 in Rock Island, exit at Seventh Avenue and go west to Fourteenth Street. Take Fourteenth Street north to the bridge to the island.

Rails to the River is a specially chartered, one-day rail tour from Chicago to the Quad Cities. The package includes rail connection, ground transportation, meals, and event admission to

Bix Jazz Festival, Bishop Hill, Village of East Davenport, Civil War Muster, Mississippi Riverboat cruise, and rail attractions. Write 3716 Fourteenth Street, Rock Island 61201 (or call 309–786–7533) for information.

Rock Island is on the site of **Black Hawk State Park,** 1510 Forty-sixth Avenue (309) 788–0177. This is the site of the westernmost battle of the Revolutionary War. On the grounds are the ◆ **Hauberg Indian Museum** and the **Watch Tower Lodge.** The museum contains a collection of Indian artifacts, paintings, and relics. A powwow is held every Labor Day. The museum has three rooms, one devoted to Black Hawk items including portraits of the chief, another devoted to the daily lives of the Sauk and Fox, and the third is a gallery of Indian chiefs and the soldiers who opposed them during the Black Hawk War.

The park is open daily from 8:00 A.M. to 10:00 P.M., and the museum and lodge are open 8:30 A.M. to 4:30 P.M.; closed for lunch from noon to 1:00 P.M. Admission is free.

The **Fryxell Geology Museum,** 639 Thirty-eighth Street, on the Augustana College campus, has a collection of fossils, which includes sauropod dinosaur eggs. Admission is free, and hours are Monday through Friday 8:00 A.M. to 5:00 P.M., Saturday and Sunday 1:00 to 4:00 P.M. Call (309) 794–1318.

The **Denkman Library,** also on campus, has the Augustana Historical Society collection of almost all the Swedish-American newspapers of North America.

Moline has a heritage of Belgian immigrants, and the ◆ **Center for Belgian Culture,** 712 Nineteenth Avenue, offers demonstrations of Belgian lace being made. Occasionally you can purchase samples. Call (309) 762–0167 for information.

A landmark in Moline is **Lagomarcino's Confectionary** at 1422 Fifth Avenue. The shop's specialty is golden sponge candy— dark chocolate coating around a crisp blond center. Everything is handmade and hand-dipped. Try the homemade ice cream and sinfully rich hot fudge sauce; (309) 764–1814.

Coal Valley is the home of the ◆ **Niabi Zoo.** Translated from the Indian, Niabi means "Spared of the Hunter's Arrow." The zoo is located on U.S. Route 6, 10 miles southeast of Moline. Besides a variety of animals, the zoo has a miniature railroad and a petting zoo designed for children. It is open April through October Wednesday, Thursday, and Friday 9:30 A.M. to 7:00 P.M.; (309) 799–5107. Admission is $3.50 for adults and $2.00 for children 4

59

to 12 years old; children under 3 are free. Tuesday is free admission for everyone. Rides on the miniature railroad are $1.00.

Quad Cities Downs is one of the Midwest's finest harness-racing facilities. Located in East Moline at Morton Drive and Route 5, racing is nightly year-round. Post time is 7:30 P.M.; call (309) 792–0202 for specific times.

Eastern Illinois

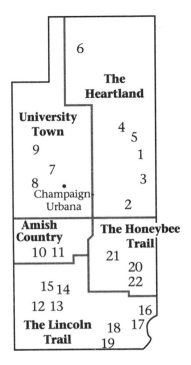

1. Kickapoo State Park
2. Grove Handicapped Trail
3. Vermilion County Museum
4. National Sweetcorn Festival
5. Aunt Jody's Christmas Bank
6. The Heartland
7. World Heritage Museum
8. Champaign County Historical Museum
9. Lake of the Woods County Park
10. Rockome Gardens
11. Arcola Emporium
12. Lincoln Log Cabin State Historic Site
13. Fox Ridge State Park
14. Eastern Illinois University
15. Coles County Courthouse
16. Lewis Home
17. Lincoln Trail State Recreation Area
18. Clark County Historical Museum
19. Richard's Farm Restaurant
20. Milton K. Alexander Home
21. Edgar County Historical Museum
22. Paris Homecoming and Honeybee Festival

Eastern Illinois

The Heartland

Illinoisans tend to whiz through Vermilion County and its county seat, Danville, along I–74 en route to Indianapolis and other points east. Why, we haven't really figured out. Besides being the easternmost big city in Illinois (apart from the *really* big one, Chicago), Danville has its charms. Among those are the area's many parks—more than 7,000 acres of parks, in fact, for only 39,000 residents, making this one of the most heavily "parked" cities in the state.

The largest is the 3,000-acre **Kennekuk Cove County Park**, where you will find the 170-acre **Lake Mingo**, which sounds like something from Flash Gordon. Actually, it's an inviting oasis where **Stephen's Beach** has all the charm of an old-fashioned swimming hole, replete with a noisy collection of boys and girls. There's fishing in the lake, too—for channel catfish, bass, and sunfish.

Follow **Lookout Point Trail** along a lush ravine system, through meadows and natural prairies. Stop to examine some of the 400 species of wildflowers, plants, and trees that grow in the park. Watch for the population of white-tailed deer and dozens of species of birds that are occasional visitors. The park's solar-heated visitor center houses an interpretive display of area Indian history. Kennekuk Cove County Park is 8 miles northwest of Danville at Henning Road off U.S. Highway 150. Park hours are 6:00 A.M. to 11:00 P.M.

What once was an ugly strip mine is today ✪ **Kickapoo State Park**, 2,843 acres of woods and ponds popular for picnicking and camping. The Middle Fork of the Vermilion River flows through the park, offering the opportunity for fishing and boating. It's a nationally designated scenic river—the only one in Illinois. Half-, one-, and two-day canoe trips begin here, with overnight accommodations either at a park campsite or—for the less adventuresome—at a hotel in Danville; (217) 354–2060. Canoes, paddles, and life vests are provided.

State park employees conduct interpretive programs year-round. In the summer there is hiking and horseback riding. The park's winter activities include ice fishing, ice skating, cross-country skiing, and sledding. Kickapoo State Park is at exit 210 off I–74. Park hours are 8:00 A.M. to 10:00 P.M.; (217) 442–4915.

In the southern part of the county, near Georgetown, **Forest Glen Preserve** is unique because of its ◆ **Grove Handicapped Trail,** paved for access by wheelchairs and said to be the only nature trail for the handicapped in the Midwest. It boasts an unusual restored tall grass prairie. Among the park flora, surprisingly, are several varieties of orchids. Also, in mid-September each year, a one-day Revolutionary War reenactment is held here, complete with pioneer homestead and camp. On I-74, take the Main Street exit right onto Route 150. At the intersection of Main and Gilbert, turn right onto Route 1. Drive into the town of Westville, turn left (east) at the stoplight. The preserve's hours are 7:00 A.M. to 11:00 P.M.

But as a major city, Danville has much more to offer than its parks. Its **Civic Center,** built in 1980, is home to entertainment year-round, ranging from pop music concerts to exhibitions to hockey games played by the local team. The Civic Center is at 100 W. Main Street; call (217) 431-2424 for information.

The ◆ **Vermilion County Museum** (116 N. Gilbert, open Tuesday through Saturday 10:00 A.M. to 5:00 P.M. and Sunday 1:00 to 5:00 P.M.) is housed in a 1850-era house, once the home of Dr. William Fithian, a friend of Abraham Lincoln. Lincoln, in fact, spoke from the balcony while running for the U.S. Senate. The bed he spent the night in is still here. The local visitors bureau acknowledges the Lincoln connection with the slogan, "We knew Abe *before* they called him Mr. President." Of special note are the doll collection in the Child's Room and the summer herb garden on the southwest corner of the grounds. The building is listed on the National Register of Historic Places. Call (217) 442-2922 for information.

The restored **Lamon House** at 1031 N. Logan in Lincoln Park is open to visitors on Sundays, May through October, or any time by appointment through the museum; (217) 442-2922. Built in 1850, it is possibly the oldest frame house extant in Danville. It is furnished with furniture of the period.

With a list of such celebrated native sons as Gene Hackman, Bobby Short, Donald O'Connor, and Dick Van Dyke, it's not surprising that the arts scene in Danville is an active one. Community theater, the Danville Light Opera, the Red Mask, and the Danville Symphony Orchestra—recently named Illinois Orchestra of the Year—provide cultural sustenance. Call the Danville Area Arts Council for information, (217) 431-6423.

For nourishment of a more basic order, country cooking is the key at **George's Buffet,** 1225 E. Voorhees. From our travels in the state, we've derived the "pickup quotient" of rating places to eat; the more pickups in the parking lot, the better the food. George's gets a sixteen-pickup rating. It's all you can eat, and with hot baked rolls, grandmother-style chicken and noodles, and a dozen or more choices, that's a lot of food. Save room for dessert. Or for something more deluxe, have dinner in one of Danville's grand historic homes, such as the **Colonel Harmon Mansion** at 522 E. Main; (217) 431–1332.

In the northern part of the county, Hoopeston and Rossville are good places to look for antiques. Hoopeston hosts the ❖ **National Sweetcorn Festival** each September. A beauty pageant, tractor pulls, and—of course—plenty of hot corn and butter are hallmarks of this event; (217) 283–7873.

Rossville, on the other hand, calls itself "the village of unusual shops," a very apt description. Along Main Street shops selling antique furniture, glass, china, primitives, and country crafts provide ample fodder for the most ambitious shopping spree. Perhaps the most unusual of these unusual shops is ❖ **Aunt Jody's Christmas Bank,** a remarkable display of nativity scenes, angels, nutcrackers, and ornaments. Open March through December; most shops closed on Mondays.

Serendipity is opening an oyster and discovering a pearl. Serendipity, too, is driving through miles of central Illinois farmland and coming upon ❖ **The Heartland.** Here in Gilman this comfortable spa is remarkably unexpected, a Thoreauvian vision of a peaceful retreat some 28 miles from Kankakee down country back roads.

The facility was once the bucolic country estate of Dr. Karl A. Meyer, former medical director of Cook County Hospital. Meyer transformed the farmland, planting thirty-one acres of woods and creating Kam Lake. When Chicagoans Gerald S. Kaufman and Charlotte Newberger bought the property in 1983, they decided to preserve much of Dr. Meyer's healthful environment and to expand upon it.

At the edge of the spring-fed lake sits the main house—Meyer's mansion—with accommodations for only twenty-seven guests and a pretty little dining room overlooking the lawn and lake. Here, too, are the Wood Room, where Heartland Institute lectures are held, and the cozy White Room for reading and conversation. An underground passageway leads to the old barn, magically transformed into a three-story fitness center with an aerobics loft, a Cam II gym, sauna, whirlpool, and massage and facial rooms. Behind it is an enclosed swimming pool.

Guests begin their stay on Friday or Sunday for either a two-day weekend or a five- or seven-day program. The all-inclusive holiday begins with a tour of the facilities and an orientation, where one of the friendly staff members explains The Heartland fitness and nutrition philosophy. Guests exchange tired big-city clothes for furnished workout togs, the uniform for all occasions throughout the stay. It's all part of the comfortable, casual attitude here.

After an optional body fat evaluation, guests move on to dinner, like all meals, a fish or vegetarian affair, beautifully presented and served. These are kosher supervised, as well. Calories are limited to 1,200 for women and 1,500 for men. Cholesterol, sodium, and fats are also limited. But no one goes hungry here. Seconds are okay, if you're not trying to lose weight. In addition to breakfast, lunch, and dinner, snacks are available at midmorning and in the afternoon. A fruit basket is always standing ready on the sideboard for those who just can't make it through. One of Chef Robert McGarrigle's menus might look like this: minestrone soup, eggplant Parmesan, steamed zucchini, fruit garnish, and carob coconut cookie. Or for lunch: Waldorf salad, frittata, green beans, and almonds.

A day's activities begin early. Wake-up comes at 7:00 A.M. (optional) followed by a morning stretch and a walk before breakfast. After the morning meal is a ninety-minute aerobics class in the fitness center where inhibitions are shed along with pounds and friendships are formed as guests struggle together through exercise class. By the end of a visit, the spirit of camaraderie is strong, along with the commitment to take home this awareness of healthy living.

Activities, it should be noted—like dance classes or horseback riding (extra fee)—are optional. So at any time you can wander away for a swim or a hike around the lake, or just take a lazy siesta in the sun with a good book. If it sounds like work, it isn't. As Director of Nutrition Susan Witz explains, rest and relaxation are among the important benefits of The Heartland, and her presentations, plus those of outside experts, address the issues of dieting and stress.

The Heartland advocates a three-part approach to stress management. The first phase, exercise, focuses on increasing body awareness. Guests explore a variety of exercise techniques. Yoga, guided relaxation, and stretching classes increase the participants' awareness of their bodies, using progressive muscle relaxation and controlled breathing.

Education is the second component of the program. Instruction here will help guests become more aware of how tensions accumulate and will introduce various attitudinal approaches, from positive thinking and calming mental imagery to improved communication strategies for defusing harmful stress.

Step three is nutrition, and the spa's balanced vegetarian menus serve that role.

Free round-trip transportation is available from Chicago. For reservations call (800) 545-4853. To reach the spa from Chicago, take the Dan Ryan Expressway south to I-57. Go 52 miles to Kankakee exit 308. Turn right at the top of the cloverleaf onto U.S. Highway 52/45 (which becomes Route 49) to U.S. Highway 24 (at the flashing red light). Turn right onto U.S. Route 24 for 2 miles to The Heartland sign and Camp Wahanaha sign (County Road 1220E). Turn left and continue for 2 miles to The Heartland sign. Turn left. The driveway to The Heartland is on the immediate right. The Heartland is 80 miles south of Chicago.

UNIVERSITY TOWN

The 56,000-student **University of Illinois,** the state's largest, shapes the landscape of the twin cities of Champaign/Urbana like nothing else. Lying at the dividing point of the two towns, the university, founded in 1867, is internationally known for its physics and engineering departments. It houses the National Center of Supercomputing Applications and is one of only five universities in this country to have a supercomputer on campus (two, in fact). It's a mecca for computer buffs.

Wander around campus and enjoy the architecture, or stop at the **Krannert Art Museum,** 500 Peabody Drive, for its collection of sculpture, old masters, and the Ewing collection of Malayan art (daily except Monday); call (217) 333-1860. Also on campus is the ◆ **World Heritage Museum,** 702 S. Wright, which exhibits the story of humankind from earliest times to modern day. Open daily except Saturday during the academic year.

Another treasure house, the **Museum of Natural History,**

1301 W. Green, is one of the finest in the Midwest, with thousands of specimens on display. It's the perfect place to take children. The Discover Room has hands-on exhibits—shells, teeth, and other artifacts—that kids can touch and examine closely. Open daily except Sunday. For the lively arts the **Krannert Center for the Performing Arts,** 500 S. Goodwin Avenue, offers a full program of dance, theater, and music throughout the year. For schedule information call (217) 333–6280. Lively sports are represented each season when Illinois plays in the Big Ten at **Memorial Stadium,** (217) 333–3470. For maps, walking tours, or directions, check in at the information desk at the Illini Union building at Wright and Green Streets; (217) 333–4666.

Other sites associated with the University of Illinois are worth a visit, too. The **Morrow Plots** at Gregory near Mathews Street in Urbana are the oldest permanent soil experiment fields in the country, in continuous use since 1876, in keeping with the original agricultural mission of the land grant school. Similarly, **three round dairy barns** built between 1902 and 1910 are part of the university's agricultural program (St. Mary's Road, Urbana). Renowned sculptor Lorado Taft studied here, graduating in 1879. **Taft's student residence,** built in 1871, is located at the Illini Grove on Pennsylvania Avenue in Urbana. One of his works, a **Lincoln statue,** sits opposite Urbana High School on Race Street.

A number of historic buildings are scattered throughout the area. The **Wilbur Mansion,** 709 W. University in Champaign, is a 1907 structure that now houses the ♦ **Champaign County Historical Museum.** Open Wednesday, Thursday, Friday, and Sunday 1:00 to 4:00 P.M.; (217) 356–1010. Also in Champaign, the **Cattle Bank Building,** 102 N. First, is the oldest remaining business building in the city, incorporated as a branch of the Grand Prairie Bank of Urbana in 1856.

In Mahomet, on Route 47, 10 miles west of Champaign/Urbana, ♦ **Lake of the Woods County Park** is a pleasant diversion in the Illinois farm country. Here, a twenty-six-acre lake with a sandy beach, canoes, rowboats, fishing, and paddleboat rentals attracts families from miles around.

They come, too, for the unique **Early American Museum and Botanical Garden,** located within the park. The museum, opened in 1968, began with the collection of local history buff William Redhead and has grown over the years. Volunteers present a fascinating series of pioneer life programs year-round—

from a colonial muster in September, to an exhibition of farm life a century ago. You might encounter a costumed interpreter making soap or stitching a quilt, dipping candles or spinning a tall folk tale. The demonstration of Christmas past is especially nice during the holidays. For children 5 to 9 years of age, Wednesday mornings in June and July mean a chance to put on a pioneer costume and spend the time just as a youngster of the 1800s might have, learning antique crafts, games, and music.

In the garden special plantings include the Heritage Garden, the Roses of Yesteryear, the Dye-Plant Garden, and a Prairie Sampler of native prairie plants. An eighteen-hole golf course, hiking trails, plus a covered bridge round out the park's attractions. Call (217) 586–3360 for information. The park is open daily year-round. Admission to the park is free. Admission to the museum is $3.00 adults; $2.00 children 11 to 17; $1.00 children 6 to 10.

Two other parks in the Champaign County Forest District are worth mentioning. **Middlefork River Forest Preserve** near Penfield has year-round camping in addition to three fishing lakes, swimming, and an activity center. The preserve is on County Road 22, about 7 miles north of Penfield; (217) 595–5432. **Salt Fork River Forest Preserve** near Homer encompasses the eighty-acre Homer Lake, popular with area fishing enthusiasts. The Trailside Visitors Center features nature displays, live animals, and educational exhibits. In early June stop by for the Salt Fork Summerfest, with nature walks, fishing demonstrations, and canoe and kayak races; (217) 896–2455. From I–74, exit at Ogden and proceed south on Route 49 for 3 miles. Turn right at the sign for the preserve onto County Road 19. The entrance to the preserve will be in 1 mile.

AMISH COUNTRY

Douglas and its neighboring county, Moultrie, are the center of Amish culture in Illinois. The first Amish in Illinois, however, came to the area around Peoria along the Illinois River in the 1830s. These early settlers immigrated from Europe—Alsace and Lorraine, Bavaria, and Hesse-Darmstadt. In the succeeding decades, though, Amish from Ohio and Pennsylvania joined those pioneers in Illinois, settling around Arcola and Arthur in the years immediately following the Civil War.

Today things haven't changed much. You can still see a plainly dressed family riding to town in a black buggy. Indeed, they are called the Plain People, for their belief in life's simple things. They eschew modern conveniences, electricity, and stylish clothes. Men dress in black or dark blue suits with "front-fall" pants (sometimes called "barn-door britches"), held up by suspenders. Shirts are of plain color and style. A flat-crowned, broadbrimmed black felt hat is worn in winter, exchanged in summer for one of straw. Amish women dress alike in almost every detail, with dresses of solid color in a pattern handed down over generations. On their heads they wear a white prayer cap covered by a black bonnet. As you drive down country back roads, you'll find horsepower of the original sort on display—Amish farmers hitched to teams of plow horses. Tractors are not used. Visiting this part of the state is a bit like stepping into a time machine, going back to a time when things were simpler.

One of the best ways to begin a trip here is a stop at ♦ **Rockome Gardens,** an amusement park 5 miles west of Arcola on Route 133. Here, on fourteen landscaped acres, nearly everything—from fences to arches to garden walls—is constructed of rocks inlaid in cement. The Gardens's **Old Bagdad Town** is a recreated frontier village with a general store, bakery, calico workshop, quilt shop, working candy shop, and a gift shop with locally made items from the Rockome Gardens Craft Guild. At the shops you can find good reproductions of Amish furniture as well. A popular feature with children is the petting zoo populated with goats, peacocks, chickens, and other farm animals. They'll also enjoy the doll shop, the tree house, and the Old Hickory Railroad. Other attractions include a "haunted" cave, a replica of an Amish home, and an antique museum. You can get in the spirit of things by taking a buggy ride around the grounds (additional fee).

A schedule of weekend festivals and special events runs all season long—from Horse Farming Days to the Quilt Show. Every September, weekends bring the Harvest Days with threshing, corn shucking, plowing demonstration (you can join in), cider pressing, and apple butter making. **Rockome Family Style Restaurant** serves up Amish-style cooking, including a wonderful shoofly pie. Admission to Rockome Gardens is $9.00 for adults, $7.00 for children 4 to 12, and $8.00 for seniors. The park is open daily from Memorial Day to Labor Day; call for the schedule during the rest of the year. The gate opens at 9:00 A.M. and closes at 5:00 P.M.; (217) 268–4216.

Amish Country

For shopping the ❖ **Arcola Emporium,** at 201 E. Main Street in downtown Arcola, offers the conveniences of a mall with a collection of charming shops selling antiques, art, women's fashions, toys, cookware, gourmet foods, and hand-crafted solid wood furniture. A number of antiques shops are also in the region.

The weekend after Labor Day, Arcola hosts the annual **Broom Corn Festival,** recalling the days when it was Broom Corn Capital of the world. A parade, a 10,000-meter road race, a flea market and street fair, plus demonstrations of broom-making, and other old-fashioned crafts, highlight the celebrations. For more information contact the Arcola Chamber of Commerce, Arcola 61910; (217) 268–3841.

THE LINCOLN TRAIL

The ❖ **Lincoln Log Cabin State Historic Site** near Charleston was the last home of Thomas and Sarah Bush Lincoln, Abraham Lincoln's parents. The cabin was built in 1837 and is now reconstructed on an eighty-six-acre lot that includes a pavilion, picnic area, and historical farm museum. The cabin is furnished with period pieces, and a kitchen building, log barn, and smokehouse from the 1840s have been added to the site. They are being restored to represent New England or "Yankee" culture in Illinois, in contrast to the Lincolns' southern upland culture.

The cabin is open 9:00 A.M. to 5:00 P.M. daily in June, July, and August, weekends 9:00 A.M. to 5:00 P.M. in May and September; (217) 345–6489. Costumed guides conduct tours during the summer, and admission is free. Special events at the cabin include the July Fourth 1845 Independence Day and Militia Muster, the Bluegrass Festival in August, the Harvest Frolic and Trades Fair in October, and the 1884 Prairie Christmas in December. You'll see signs for the site on Fourth Street Road, 8 miles south of Charleston.

❖ **Fox Ridge State Park** is 8 miles south of Charleston on Route 130. A wooded tract with rolling hills running along the Embarras River, the park has fishing, boating, hiking, picnicking, and camping. For information contact the Park Manager, R.R. 1, Box 234, Charleston 62910; (217) 345–6416.

The **Shiloh Cemetery** is located about 1½ miles southwest of Campbell, along the Lincoln Heritage Trail. Previously called Gordon's Cemetery, it is the resting place of Thomas and Sarah Bush Lincoln. When historians discovered Thomas Lincoln's cabin and began to restore it, the citizens of Coles County dedicated themselves to perpetuating the gravesite. It is also a major cemetery for Civil War veterans.

A few miles north of the Lincoln Cabin on the Lincoln Heritage Trail is the **Moore House** in Campbell. It was the home of Rueben and Matilda Moore. Matilda was the daughter of Sarah Bush Lincoln and was Abraham Lincoln's stepsister. In January 1861 Lincoln paid his last visit to Coles County and his stepsister at this home. The grounds of the home are open to the public.

The **Stephen Sargent Farm** is located 10 miles south of the Lincoln Cabin. It is open to the public when staffing permits. It is a fine example of progressive farming of the 1840s. This is in contrast to the Lincoln Farm, which exemplifies subsistence farming. For more information contact the Lincoln Log Cabin State Historic Site, R.R. 1, Box 172A, Herma 62440 or call (217) 345–6489.

The **Indian Church** is 3½ miles west of the Lincoln Heritage

71

Trail between County Roads 1150E and 250N. This was the first church built on the Little Indian Creek in 1832.

The **5-Miles House** at the corner of Route 130 and the West-field Road (about 5 miles southeast of Coles County Courthouse in Charleston) was built in 1836. It was originally a wayside tavern and a place to water and care for horses. In 1849 it was an outfitting shop for travelers to the gold fields. It now contains a display of contemporary implements in front of the house (now a private residence).

❖ **Eastern Illinois University** is the cultural center of Coles County. The battlements of Old Main, an example of German Gothic architecture, tower over the campus. The museum and greenhouses of the Life Science Building are open to the public. Various artworks are on display in the lobby of the Fine Arts Building, and the **Paul Sargent Art Gallery** is in the Booth Library. The **Tarble Arts Center** displays fine art and has changing exhibits. Check with the university for hours; (217) 581–5000. Admission is free.

The university sponsors a **Celebration in Arts Festival** the last weekend in April. Call (217) 581–5000 for information.

A **replica of the Liberty Bell** became part of Charleston's heritage during the Bicentennial celebration of 1976. The bell hangs in Morton Park on Lincoln Street (Route 16).

The ❖ **Coles County Courthouse,** built in 1898, was remodeled in 1951. Located in Charleston's town square, it is where Lincoln practiced law, and it is the scene of the Charleston Riot, which involved 300 men in an armed conflict during the Civil War. The Will Rogers Movie Theater, 705 Monroe Street, named after the comedian and philosopher, is an example of art deco architecture and is listed on the National Register of Historic Places.

The fourth Lincoln-Douglas debate was held in Charleston on September 8, 1858. The site of the debate is now the **Coles County Fairgrounds** on Route 316 on the west end of Charleston. A display of the debate and six other historic debates, replicas of historic documents relating to the debates, and a stone marker commemorate the site.

East of the debate site are the **Old Cemetery** and **Chambers Cemetery.** Here are the graves of Col. and Mrs. Augustus C. Chapman and Mr. and Mrs. Dennis Friend Hanks, relatives of Lincoln. Hanks supposedly taught Lincoln to read and write.

There are also graves of many of the early settlers, including Charles Morton, founder of Charleston.

Charleston and Coles County celebrate a variety of festivals. In July Charleston has its nineteenth-century trade fair. More than a dozen tradespeople, dressed in period clothing, demonstrate such trades as tinsmithing, blacksmithing, woodworking, tailoring, and shoemaking. The weekend of activities is held at the Lincoln Log Cabin State Historical Site from 10:00 A.M. to 5:00 P.M.

In July the 1845 Militia Muster presents a reenactment of early Illinois militia training with weekend drills, shooting competitions, and military inspections. A mock battle is the highlight of Sunday. This is also at the Lincoln Log Cabin site.

For information on the festivals, contact the Charleston Chamber of Commerce, 501 Jackson Street, P.O. Box 99, Charleston 61920; (217) 345-7041.

Although primarily an agricultural county, Clark County has two literary associations worth noting. James Jones, author of *From Here to Eternity*, made his home in Marshall, the county seat. Indiana writer Booth Tarkington visited Marshall often as a boy and then recounted those experiences in his nostalgic novel, *Penrod*.

The town of about 4,000 has a wealth of charm that could easily serve as writerly inspiration—quiet streets with leafy canopies of oak and maple, solid turn-of-the-century brick homes. One of the best examples is the 1908 ◆ **Lewis Home,** 503 Chestnut, with its dramatic two-story columned veranda (listed in the National Register of Historic Places, but not open to public inspection). The old-fashioned bandstand at the county courthouse is home to the oldest continuing city band in the state. The band, with a century-long history, performs every Friday night on the courthouse lawn from the end of May through August.

The original inhabitants of the county were the Kickapoo Indians, who ceded the land to the United States government in 1819. By 1832 they had been moved from the area. A year later the site on which Marshall was built was purchased by Col. William Archer and Joseph Duncan, later the sixth governor of Illinois. The town was named after the fourth chief justice of the United States, John Marshall.

Like the eastern states, which are dotted with spots that claim "George Washington slept (or ate or visited or whatever) here," we in Illinois have the Lincoln legend at every turn. The **Lincoln**

The Lewis Home

Heritage Trail, created in 1963, marks the route the family traveled from their original home in Kentucky, through Indiana, to Macon County, Illinois. Here in Clark County, the ◆ **Lincoln Trail State Recreation Area** marks the area through which the Lincolns passed in 1830 on their way to a new home in Decatur. The 146-acre Lincoln Trail Lake is its focal point. The park offers camping (electricity, showers, and toilets available), fishing (bass, bluegill, crappie, channel catfish), picnicking, and hiking on trails up to 2 miles long. Boats are available for rental. In the winter enjoy ice fishing, ice skating, and cross-country skiing. For information contact the Site Superintendent's office, (217) 826–2222. The recreation area is 2 miles south of Marshall on Route 1; then drive 1 mile west.

    Mill Creek Park, 7 miles northwest of Marshall, is operated by the Clark County Park District, the first county park district to be formed in Illinois (1967). The 2,600-acre park encloses Mill Creek Lake, an 811-acre flood control reservoir. The park opened in 1982. The campground has 192 sites (electric hookups available). Fees are $12 per night. For reservations write Clark County Park District, R.R. 2, Marshall 62441, or phone (217) 889–3601.

74

Besides fishing for bass, walleye, catfish, crappie, and bluegill, sample the equestrian or RV trails and the picnicking and swimming areas in the park. Mill Creek Park is on the Lincoln Heritage Trail 1 mile west of Clarksville.

In Marshall visit the ◆ **Clark County Historical Museum,** 502 S. Front Street, built in 1833 as the home of early postmaster Uri Manly. The museum is open free of charge on Sunday 1:00 to 4:00 P.M. during the summer. At the First Methodist Church, the **Hinners Track Action Pipe Organ** dates from 1909. Find these sights on the walking tour sponsored by the Marshall Area Chamber of Commerce. Write for a brochure: 708 Archer Avenue, P.O. Box 263, Marshall 62441; phone (217) 826–2034.

Casey, on U.S. Highway 40 at Clark County's western border, is famous for ◆ **Richard's Farm Restaurant,** which is situated in an old barn. The specialty of the house is a one-pound pork chop. Enjoy the decor and a seat in the hayloft and perhaps a chat with owners Diane and Gary Richards. Open daily for lunch and dinner; (217) 932–5300. Dinners range from $10 to $16. The restaurant is 1 block east of the intersection of Route 49 and U.S. Highway 40.

Plan a visit for Saturday night and take in Casey's famous **Saturday Night Auction,** held weekly at 5:30 P.M., with collectibles from area shops and individuals. It's held at the auction house in downtown Casey on Route 49; (217) 932–6186. Or stop by the auction house's salesroom any day from 8:00 A.M. to 4:00 P.M.

THE HONEYBEE TRAIL

This may be Illinois's most international county, with a Paris, Scotland, Palermo, and even a Kansas within its borders. The county seat, Paris, lies in the heart of a rich farming area. Both Paris and the county date from 1823 when pioneer Samuel Vance donated twenty-six acres. Today's wonderfully ornate **county courthouse** (listed in the National Register of Historic Places) sits at the center of that land. Vance laid out many of the county's earliest roads, some still traveled today. The county seat gets its name from settlers arriving from Paris, Kentucky, it is believed. Forty years later those southern settlers sympathized with the Confederacy during the Civil War and came to be known as Copperheads. When first established, Edgar County extended north all the way to Lake Michigan. Paris was incorporated as a village in 1849.

75

A number of historic homes grace this lovely little town. The
◆ **Milton K. Alexander Home,** at 130 S. Central Avenue, was
the residence of a brigadier general in the Illinois Mounted Volunteers during the Black Hawk War of 1832. The house was built
in 1826, with additions in 1840. It is now home to the **Bicentennial Art Center,** open noon to 4:00 P.M. Tuesday through
Friday and 1:00 to 3:00 P.M. Saturday and Sunday; (217) 466–8130.

The **Daniel Arthur Home,** 414 N. Main Street, was built in
1872 and now houses the ◆ **Edgar County Historical
Museum.** Open Wednesday and Sunday afternoons 1.30 to 4.00
P.M.. For more information call (217) 463–5305.

Each year at the end of September, the town is abuzz with the
excitement of the annual ◆ **Paris Homecoming and Honeybee Festival.** Known as the honeybee capital of the nation, the
community features the best-known product as well as arts and
crafts, an antique car show, and a parade. Concurrently, the
museum sponsors **Prairie Settler Day,** with exhibits and
demonstrations of pioneer life. Call the Paris Chamber of Commerce for further information, (217) 465–4179.

Twin Lakes Park, the largest of ten in the city, offers camping (tent or RV, toilets, showers, electric hookups), boating, fishing, picnic areas, and cooking grills. The star attraction of West
Lake is a small amusement park. The park is on the northern edge
of the city on Route 1 and U.S. Highway 50; (217) 465–7601.

Palermo, in the northwest corner of the county, is the site of a
historic meeting and peace council between Ottawa Indian Chief
Pontiac and George Croghan, the British deputy superintendent
of Indian Affairs. The 1765 parley settled the uprising known as
Pontiac's Conspiracy, which occurred shortly after the French
and Indian War.

CENTRAL ILLINOIS

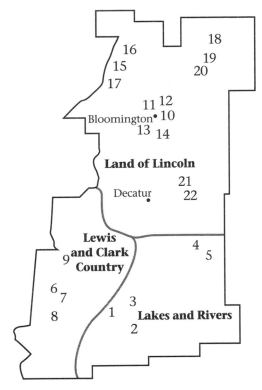

16
15
17
18
19
20

11 12
Bloomington• 10
13 14

Land of Lincoln

21
Decatur• 22

Lewis and Clark Country
9

4 5

6
7
8

3
1 **Lakes and Rivers**
2

1. Ramsey Lake State Fish and Wildlife Area
2. Vandalia Statehouse
3. Lake Shelbyville
4. Little Theatre on the Square
5. Ward's Museum
6. Lewis and Clark State Park
7. Cahokia Mounds
8. Stone memorial to Lovejoy
9. Million Dollar Courthouse
10. Lincoln College
11. Museum of the Presidents
12. Atlanta Public Library and Museum

13. John Dean Gillett Memorial Chapel
14. Mount Pulaski Courthouse
15. Everett McKinley Dirksen Congressional Leadership Center
16. Fond du Lac Park
17. Fort Creve Coeur State Park
18. Tropical Rain Forest
19. Adlai E. Stevenson I Home
20. Dewitt County Museum
21. Scoville Children's Zoo
22. Mari-Mann Herb Farm and Gingerbread House

CENTRAL ILLINOIS
LAKES AND RIVERS

Illinois may be known for its cornfields, but beginning in the central part of the state, lakes and rivers abound.

The area around ❖ **Ramsey Lake State Fish and Wildlife Area** was originally called Old Fox Chase Grounds and was popular with fox and raccoon hunters. It was first considered as a public recreation area in the late 1920s during the administration of Gov. Len Small. In 1947 the state of Illinois purchased 815 acres for a lake site, and additional land acquisition increased the area to 1,880 acres.

Ramsey Lake is 1 mile northwest of Ramsey off U.S. Highway 51 in a rolling, wooded terrain. The lake was constructed in a valley with an elevated timbered shoreline of almost 4 miles.

Ramsey Lake has fishing, hunting, camping, picnicking, hiking, horseback riding, and snowmobiling facilities. **White Oak Campground** has 100 sites with a sanitary disposal station, electric hookups, flush toilets, and shower building. Two other campgrounds have more rugged facilities. Reservations are available from the site staff.

There are several picnic shelters, which have water, tables, and stoves. Fox Knoll, Coon Ridge, and Blackberry Fork picnic areas are small, shady, secluded knolls that overlook the lake.

Hikers will find a 1-mile designated trail and several miles of unmarked land.

The lake is stocked with largemouth bass, bluegill, redear sunfish, channel catfish, and black crappie. Boats can be rented, but only electric trolling motors are allowed. Fishing is also allowed in the small ponds. Check with the park office for catch and size limits on fish.

The horse trail, at the north end, is 13 miles long. A small equestrian campground is 1 mile north of the park entrance.

Dove, squirrel, quail, pheasant, and deer hunting are permitted in season, deer hunting only with a bow. Shotguns only are permitted, and no hunting is allowed inside of Lake Circle Drive.

Ice fishing, snowmobiling, cross-country skiing, sledding, and ice skating are permitted in winter.

For information and reservations contact the Site Superintendent, Ramsey Lake State Fish and Wildlife Area, P.O. Box 97, Ramsey 62080; (618) 423–2215.

Vandalia was the second capital of Illinois, but it was the first capital in the state to build a statehouse from scratch.

The first Illinois statehouse was a rented building in Kaskaskia. It was the seat of state government from 1818 to 1820. When the capital was moved to Vandalia, a two-story frame building was rented and the first session of the Second General Assembly met here on December 4, 1820. On December 9, 1823, fire destroyed the building.

The State Bank Building was remodeled and repaired and became the new statehouse. In spite of the repairs, the building was still in poor condition. It was so unsound that by 1836, no one dared hold a meeting there for fear of the building collapsing.

In August 1836 Gov. Joseph Duncan authorized Auditor Levi Davis to either have the building repaired, rent an assembly hall, or build a new statehouse. It was decided to forget the old plans and build a new statehouse in the style of vernacular Federal architecture.

A bill of $16,378.22 was presented to the legislature for the building. The legislature appropriated $10,378.22 and Duncan drew $5,500 more from the contingency fund. The balance was contributed by individuals. The total cost of the building was $23,241.45.

Some of the important issues discussed at the ◆ **Vandalia Statehouse** were slavery and the establishment of Illinois as a free state. The first school laws of Illinois were enacted here and the controversial State Bank was debated here. The city of Chicago was also incorporated by the 1836–37 legislature, which included Stephen A. Douglas and Abraham Lincoln.

As the population shifted proposals were made to move the capital. On February 18, 1837, the General Assembly voted to move the capital to Springfield.

In 1933 the Illinois Department of Conservation began restoration of the statehouse. At 315 W. Gallatin, it is open daily to visitors from 9:00 A.M. to 5:00 P.M. year-round except Thanksgiving, Christmas, and New Year's Day. Admission is free, and guided tours are available. For information call (618) 283–1161.

Shelby County is blessed with natural resources set aside for public recreation. Within its boundaries lie Hidden Springs, Wolf

Creek, and Eagle Creek state parks; Lake Mattoon; Lake Pana; and—most importantly— ❖ **Lake Shelbyville.** This giant lake is one of the state's largest, covering 11,100 acres with 172 miles of wooded shoreline protected from development by the U.S. Army Corps of Engineers. It reaches 20 miles from Shelbyville, the county seat in the south, to Sullivan in Moultrie County in the north.

Begun in 1963 and completed in 1970 as a flood control project, the lake contains the Kaskaskia and Okaw Rivers. Today the recreational benefits are primary on the minds of most visitors, with camping, boating, fishing, picnicking, hiking, and swimming all available to weekend adventurers. Call (217) 774–2020 for recorded lake fishing conditions. Your catch might be white or largemouth bass, walleye, crappie, channel catfish, northern pike, or any of two dozen or so varieties of fish found in the lake.

There are only three marinas on the lake—Fox Harbor in Moultrie County and Lithia Springs and Findlay in Shelby County. Lithia Springs is closest to Shelbyville and boasts a modest motel, the **Lithia Resort,** only a short walk away. An alternative accommodation choice, however, is offered in the houseboat rental. Lithia rents spacious houseboats by the week or portion of week for prices ranging from $500 to $1,125; (217) 774–4121. For that you can bring six or eight people and make it a party. To reach Lithia Springs Marina, drive 3 miles east of Shelbyville on Route 16; then turn north and follow the signs.

Sailboats and fishing boats, water-skiers, and naturalists happily coexist on the lake where deep forested coves seem far away from the flat farmland not too distant. On shore, campers will find more than 500 campsites with electrical hookups. During the summer season Corps of Engineer personnel present a schedule of interpretive programs on a range of spiffy topics: "Family Water Safety," "Through an Insect's Eye," "Wild Edible Plants," and others. Be sure to stop at the visitors center at the **Dam East Recreation Area,** 1 mile east of Shelbyville on Route 16 (open Memorial Day through Labor Day), which offers audio-visual programs, exhibits, and an unmatched view of the dam.

Apart from the lake there's plenty to see ashore. In Shelbyville, named for Revolutionary War Gen. Isaac Shelby, drive up Washington Street to view the handsome Civil War–era homes. Downtown the French Second Empire-style **county courthouse** is a local point of interest. The old, multisided **Chautauqua Audito-**

80

rium in Forest Park dates from the period around 1903 when evangelist Jasper L. Douthit held his celebrated religious meetings here.

Although farming may be the primary enterprise in Moultrie County, fishing is probably the primary pastime. Sullivan, the county seat, advertises itself as the "northern gateway to beautiful Lake Shelbyville." It shares the 11,000-acre lake with Shelby County to the south. So at the same time that the county claims first place in statewide corn-per-acre production, its production of walleye, crappie, and largemouth bass isn't bad either.

If you're camping, try **Sullivan's Marina and Campground,** south of town on Lake Shelbyville; (217) 728–7338. There are boat rentals and plenty of wooded terrain just across from the **Sullivan Recreation Area,** which has a well-maintained swimming beach.

Sullivan is situated on the Lincoln Heritage Trail. It claims to be the only town with a National Guard unit once commanded by Abraham Lincoln. Less honorably, it was also the scene of a near-riot on the day that both Lincoln and Douglas were in town to give speeches.

The ◆ **Little Theatre on the Square** is the town's pride and joy and Sullivan's claim to summer culture fame. Founded in 1957, it bills itself as the only professional equity theater between Chicago and St. Louis. And each year from the end of May through mid-August, a program of musicals and plays is presented by the Little Theatre's own company; (217) 728–7375.

On the north side of town, **Wyman Park** and **Wyman Lake** make up forty acres of recreational area offering tennis, a playground, and room for picnicking. Nearby the **Civic Center** has an Olympic-size indoor heated pool with diving area, racquetball courts, and a gymnasium.

Also in town is **The Depot,** an antiques shop with a split personality—one store a chock-full antique mall, and across the tracks, a gallery. Hours are Monday through Saturday, 10:00 A.M. to 5:00 P.M.

Just outside of town, east on Route 121, is the **Illinois Masonic Home.** Land for the home was given before the century by Mason Robert A. Miller upon which to build a residence for Masons and their widows. The first building was dedicated in 1904. Today more than 300 retired persons reside here. Its beautiful grounds include a deer park, a landscaped lake, and a greenhouse that furnishes fresh flowers daily for the home. A small

81

collection called ◆ **Ward's Museum** is housed in the main building. Open to the public, it includes 10,000 specimens of seashells, plus primitive furniture and other antiques. In a separate building is an old-fashioned ice cream parlor complete with a marvelous player piano. Visitors are welcome at the home year-round; (217) 728–4394. Hours are 8:00 A.M. to 4:30 P.M. Monday through Friday, 8:00 A.M. to 4:00 P.M. Saturday and Sunday. No admission charge.

LEWIS AND CLARK COUNTRY

Commemorating the starting point of the famous expedition to the Pacific Coast is ◆ **Lewis and Clark State Park** in Madison County. South of Wood River on Route 3, 2 miles north of I–270, the monument to the expedition consists of eleven concrete pylons that form the rotunda and represent the eleven Trail States traversed by the expedition. Individual plaques briefly review the party's activities as it traveled cross county.

The ◆ **Cahokia Mounds** in Collinsville are recognized as a World Heritage site by the United Nations Educational, Scientific, and Cultural Organization (UNESCO). The site has changed from a camping, picnic, and playground facility into a valuable international cultural resource. The site and Museum Society offer educational programs and publications. There is also a gift and book shop. Take I–55/70 to exit 11 at Route 157, then south to U.S. Highway 40, then west to Cahokia Mounds World Heritage Site.

The main feature are the sixty-five intact mounds. Originally there were approximately 120 mounds and most were ceremonial. **Monk's Mound** is the largest prehistoric mound north of Mexico. The museum is open daily from 9:00 A.M. to 5:00 P.M. except on major holidays.

Edwardsville, at the center of the county, boasts two areas listed on the National Historic Register—the **St. Louis Street Historic District** and the **LeClaire Historic District,** as well as the handsome campus of **Southern Illinois University** at Edwardsville.

Horseshoe Lake State Park on 2,600 acres on Route 111, west of Edwardsville, offers a wide variety of family fun: picnicking, boating, fishing, hunting, camping, bird-watching, and cross-country skiing. The area was inhabited by Indian groups, with the earliest evidence dating from 8000 B.C. during the Archaic Period. Artifacts have been found that fall into the Woodland Period, 1000

Monks Mound at Cahokia Mounds

B.C. to A.D. 1000. The park is open year-round except for holidays. Contact the Site Superintendent, Horseshoe Lake State Park, P.O. Box 1307, Granite City 62040; (618) 931–0270.

Turf enthusiasts will savor the excitement at the **Fairmount Park Race Track** on Route 140 in Collinsville. Both harness and thoroughbred racing are on the bill from January through November.

For an unusual event Collinsville sponsors an annual **Horseradish Festival.** Contact the Collinsville Chamber of Commerce, 221 W. Main Street, Collinsville 62234, (618) 344–2884, for more information.

Alton was the site of **Alton Prison,** the state's first penitentiary. The remnants of a cell block wall have been restored as a monument to this primitive penitentiary, which housed Confederate prisoners during the Civil War. The **penitentiary monument** is at the corner of Broadway and Williams Streets near downtown Alton.

The town's colorful history includes Rev. Elijah P. Lovejoy, a newspaperman who crusaded against slavery and was shot down by a hostile mob. He was shot on November 8, 1837, and sixty years later, a 90-foot ❖ **stone memorial to Lovejoy**—the tallest memorial in the state—was erected near his grave. In 1915 the frame of his printing press went on display in the lobby of the Alton Telegraph Building.

Carlinville is home to the ❖ **Million Dollar Courthouse,** more affectionately termed the "White Elephant." The courthouse was far beyond the needs of the county and cost much more than anticipated when construction began in 1867. Within a few months the building commissioners and the county court knew that the building would be more than double the $150,000 estimated cost.

It was 2½ years before the building was finished and forty years before it was paid for. When it was finally completed, the move from the old courthouse to the new was quietly made. The eventual cost was $1,300,000.

The building is made of limestone and consists of two rectangles that cross at the center and are surmounted with a dome. The dome rises 191 feet above the street, and 40-foot columns support the roof. Every door is made of iron, and each outer door weighs more than a ton. All interior trim is of iron or stone. The judge's chair, costing $1,500, is mounted on a track behind the varicolored marble bench.

Macoupin County Historical Museum has a collection of county historical items; a music room with an old grand piano; exhibits of furniture, pottery, china, and glass; stained glass windows from a German exhibitor at the 1893 World's Fair in Chicago; an 1890 bathroom; and memorabilia of early Macoupin County doctors. The museum celebrates three special events: a Strawberry Festival the last weekend in May, a Fall Festival the third weekend in September, and special holiday decorations for the Christmas season.

A gift shop on the premises carries postcards, county history reprints, and craft items. Hours are April through November, Wednesday 10:00 A.M. to 2:00 P.M., June through August, Sunday 1:00 to 5:00 P.M. Admission is $2.00 for adults, $1.00 for children 6 to 16, no charge for children under 6. The museum is on Breckenridge Road in Carlinville; (217) 854–2850.

LAND OF LINCOLN

Local residents say, "Lincoln never lived here, but he left a lot of tracks." Abraham Lincoln christened Logan County, owned property here, practiced law at the Eighth Judicial Circuit Court at Mount Pulaski, and his funeral train stopped here.

Logan County was a result of Abraham Lincoln's efforts to divide Sangamon County into four smaller counties in 1839. At his suggestion one of the counties was named after Dr. John Logan, a friend of Lincoln's who was instrumental in helping persuade the legislature to move the state capital to Springfield.

The town of Lincoln is the only one named with his knowledge and consent. The honor evolved from three partners in Postville, engaging Lincoln as a lawyer to establish joint ownership of the tract of land near Postville. The partners decided to name the town Lincoln, against the advice of Lincoln himself. He said, "Never knew anything named Lincoln that amounted to much."

Customized tours of Lincoln are available from the Abraham Lincoln Tourism Bureau of Logan County at no charge and by appointment only. Phone (217) 732–8687 (TOUR).

Other historical events involving Abraham Lincoln include his and Stephen A. Douglas's visit to the area during their senatorial campaign in the summer of 1858. On November 21, 1859, Lincoln gave a farewell address to the citizens here, and on May 3, 1865, his funeral train was greeted with mourners singing hymns and paying their last respects.

The **Lincoln Gallery,** 111 N. Sangamon, has a statue of Lincoln christening the town. Lloyd Ostendorf's oil paintings depict Lincoln's life in Logan County, Washington, D.C., and Gettysburg. They are inside the Olympia Savings and Loan Association building. Hours are Monday through Wednesday 8:30 A.M. to 3:00 P.M., Thursday 8:30 A.M. to noon, Friday 8:30 A.M. to 5:00 P.M., and Saturday 8:30 A.M. to noon.

✦ **Lincoln College** was established in 1865 with the donation of ten acres of land by John D. Gillett and Robert B. Latham, two of the founding fathers. The cornerstone of the **University Hall** was laid on February 12, 1865, Lincoln's last living birthday. The hall is listed in the National Register of Historic Places.

The McKinstry Library, on campus, houses the ✦ **Museum of the Presidents,** an outstanding collection of more than

2,500 Lincoln artifacts. The **Merrill Gage Statue** showing Lincoln as a student is also on campus.

Lincoln Rustic, 412 Pulaski Street, is the site where a conspiracy developed to steal Lincoln's body from Oak Ridge Cemetery in Springfield.

The **Postville Courthouse,** 914 Fifth Street, is open Friday and Saturday from 9:00 A.M. to 5:00 P.M. (217–732–8930), and it was here that Lincoln received his nickname "Honest Abe." The building was completed in 1840, and Lincoln served here as a member of the bar for a quarter of a century. The building was reconstructed in 1953; the original stands in Greenfield Village, Michigan.

Another site of interest in Logan County is the ❖ **Atlanta Public Library and Museum,** Race Street, Atlanta (217–648–2112). The museum contains artifacts from the area, and the building is actually Logan County's first bank. The library is listed in the National Register of Historic Places and is one of only a few octagonal-plan libraries in Illinois. Hours are Tuesday through Saturday, 12:30 to 4:30 P.M.

The **Middletown Stage Coach Inn** in Middletown was established in 1832 and still stands. Middletown is believed to be the oldest town in Logan County and served as a midpoint and stagecoach stop on the Peoria-Springfield Road. The **bank building** in Middletown is thought to be the oldest building in Logan County.

Elkhart Cemetery in Elkhart has the ❖ **John Dean Gillett Memorial Chapel,** a charming country chapel that is privately owned and self-supporting. It was built in 1890 and erected in memory of John Dean Gillett, the "Cattle King of America."

Richard S. Oglesby, three-time governor of Illinois, is also buried in this cemetery. Oglesby was the person who nominated Lincoln for the presidency and was the first to call him the "Railsplitter." The **Logan Railsplitting Festival** is held the second weekend after Labor Day. This is a nineteenth-century-style festival featuring a railsplitting contest, flea market, food, and entertainment. Contact the Logan Railsplitting Festival and Association, P.O. Box 352, Lincoln 62656; (217) 732–4795.

Mount Pulaski was named for Count Casimir Pulaski, a Polishborn soldier who joined the Continental army of George Washington in 1777. The ❖ **Mount Pulaski Courthouse** is Greek Revival architecture and one of the two surviving courthouses from Lincoln's days in the Eighth Judicial Circuit Court. It is located in the town's square and is open daily from 9:00 A.M. to 5:00 P.M.

Pekin, once a major port on the Illinois River during the steamboat era, is one of the oldest settlements in Tazewell County. Like many other towns in western Illinois, it was visited by Abraham Lincoln and was used as a fort during the Black Hawk War.

Pekin is also the home of the ◆ **Everett McKinley Dirksen Congressional Leadership Center,** the nation's only educational institution devoted to the study of congressional leadership. The center is located at Broadway and Fourth Streets. It contains the late senator's office files, speeches, audio and visual tapes, records, photographs, books, and memorabilia. The major exhibit is "Congress: The Voice of the People." This exhibit shows examples of how the citizenry participates in the legislative process.

In addition to the Exhibition Hall, the center has a growing collection of memorabilia relating to Congress. Senator Dirksen began the collection with contributions of his own artwork, sculpture, photographs, flags, letters, and political mementos. These objects are used in special exhibits.

Visitors can tour the Exhibition Hall and also view special programs offered in the Assembly Room. These programs must be arranged by advance request. Admission is free, and the museum is open to the public Monday through Friday 9:00 A.M. to 5:00 P.M. Additional winter hours are Saturday 10:00 A.M. to 4:00 P.M., September through May; (309) 347–7113.

The Pekin area lies at the boundary between the Bloomington Ridge Plain that was formed by Wisconsin glaciers nearly 22,000 years ago and the Springfield Plain formed by the Illinoisan glaciers about 200,000 years ago. The geological history of the Mississippi and Illinios Rivers can be studied through field trips sponsored by the Illinois Department of Energy and Natural Resources, State Geological Survey Division, Natural Resources Building, 615 E. Peabody Drive, Champaign 61820. Call (217) 344–1481 for information.

In mid-September Pekin holds its **Annual Marigold Festival** to celebrate the flower that blooms throughout the city. A parade and art fair are part of the celebration. Contact the Pekin Chamber of Commerce, 116 S. Capitol, P.O. Box 636, Pekin 61554, (309) 346–2106, for a list of activities.

The **Spring Lake State Conservation Area**—1 mile south of Pekin on Route 29, 9 miles southwest on Manito Blacktop and 3 miles west on Spring Lake Blacktop—is a 1,996-acre park with a fish hatchery and fishing, boating, hiking, cross-country skiing, and picnicking facilities. Contact the Park Manager, R.R. 1, Box 248, Manito 61546, (309) 968–7135, for information.

East Peoria, at the base of the bluffs on the floodplain of the Illinois River, is the home of **McGlothlin Farm Park.** Located on Neumann Drive off Meadows Avenue at U.S. Highway 150, the park is a picture of farm life. It has duck ponds, a schoolhouse, barn, brooder, blacksmith shop, and hen house. Animals on the farm are typical of those on many area farms and are free to roam the grounds. Visitors are allowed to pet and feed them. For information call (309) 694–2195.

The **General Store,** on the grounds of the park, offers a variety of toys, country items, and candy. The **Country Kitchen** is open to view antiques, and when a special event is scheduled, baked goods are baked in an old woodstove on the premises. Concessions as well as picnic tables are available. Summer hours are 10:00 A.M. to 5:00 P.M. Tuesday through Saturday and 1:00 to 6:00 P.M. Sunday. Closed mid-October to May 1. Admission is $1.50 for adults, $1.00 for children.

◆ **Fond du Lac Park** at Springfield and Steward Avenues in East Peoria has an extensive view of Peoria and the Illinois River Valley. Its more than 2,000 acres on the east bank of the Illinois River offer picnic areas, hiking, golf, tennis, camping, and swimming facilities. Call (309) 699–3923.

◆ **Fort Creve Coeur State Park** in Creve Coeur was once the site of explorer LaSalle's outpost. The fort, established in 1680, was ill-fated. It was a proposed base for exploration and colonization of the Mississippi Valley, but when LaSalle went to Quebec and left another man in charge, the dissatisfied troops destroyed the fort and went into the wilderness with all the powder and provisions. The fort was never rebuilt. A granite marker commemorates the founding of the fort and tells the story of its desertion.

The **Fort Creve Coeur Rendezvous** is an annual event held the fourth weekend in September. The festivities feature voyageurs with canoes, buckskin-garbed troops, flintlocks, and crafts. Contact Fort Creve Coeur State Park at (309) 694–3193 for dates and information.

At the heart of the Illinois prairie sit the sister cities of Bloomington and Normal. The earliest records show the first white people were here around 1800—traders and trappers who made a living roaming the region bordering the Mississippi River. A local legend says that one such group hid a keg of whiskey here in a thick grove of trees, only to have it discovered by an Indian party that finished it off handily. Thus, when the first settlers arrived in 1822, the place was called Keg Grove. Seven years later, when the first post office was established, the settlement called itself Blooming Grove for the area's profusion of flowers.

McLean County was organized in 1830; a year later, Bloomington, laid out on 22½ acres donated by James Allin just north of Blooming Grove, was designated the county seat. Normal, once North Bloomington, takes it name from what was the State Normal University, now Illinois State University (founded in 1857). Bloomington's university, Illinois Wesleyan, was chartered in 1853. Apart from being university towns and a center of county government, the communities have a rich business and industrial base. For example, the home office of State Farm Insurance Company is based here.

History and politics have long been intertwined here, as well. Some say Bloomington's David Davis was the man who "made Lincoln president." A noted lawyer and member of the state legislature, Davis was elected judge of the Eighth Judicial Circuit in 1848, a position that put him in frequent contact with the lawyer Abraham Lincoln. At the 1860 Republican Convention, Davis worked behind the scenes to organize support for Illinois's favorite son. In 1862 Lincoln rewarded him with an appointment to the Supreme Court. Davis was elected to the U.S. Senate in 1877.

His mansion, **Clover Lawn,** is one of the top attractions for visitors. A state historic site, the twenty-room Italian villa includes much of the original furnishings from the 1872 period. The house is built of yellow-faced brick with stone quoins in the corners. Its tower rises 50 feet above the ground. Inside, eight marble fireplaces decorate rooms done in high Victorian style, a fine example of upper-class life of the period. The home is open from 9:00 A.M. to 4:00 P.M. daily except Tuesdays and Wednesdays and major holidays. Admission is free. Call for further details; (309) 828–1084.

Another mansion *cum* museum is the **Ewing Manor Cultural Center,** the former home of Hazel Buck Ewing, whose father was associated with William Wrigley, Jr., in the foundation of the Wrigley Company of Chicago. Also known as the Ewing Castle, the 1929 estate is done in the style of a Norman castle. Upon the death of the wealthy philanthropist, the property became part of the Illinois State University Foundation. It's not open to the public, but drive by and enjoy the architecture. Emerson Street at Towanda Avenue.

In July and early August, the **Illinois Shakespeare Festival** presents three Shakespearean plays here in repertory nightly Tuesday through Sunday. Picnicking on the lawn of the Ewing Manor is especially popular with festival-goers; (309) 438–2535.

The **McLean County Historical Society Museum** catalogues the county's past with exhibits of Indian artifacts, decorative arts, military souvenirs, and crafts. Upstairs there's a neat gift shop and genealogy collection. One of the star attractions is the **"Tilbury Flash,"** a 1930s racing plane built in Bloomington, among the smallest in the world. Special shows are mounted throughout the year. The museum is open daily at various hours; call for details. Tuesdays admission is free; the remainder of the week it's $2.00 for adults and $1.00 for children 12 and under. The museum is housed in the old McLean County Courthouse at 200 N. Main Street; (309) 827–0428.

At the McLean County Fairground in Bloomington, the **Third Sunday Market** is like an attic full of collectibles and antiques. Show admission is $3.00; parking is free. For information phone (309) 452–7926. The monthly event is managed by Don and Carol Raycraft, authorities and authors on country antiques.

Illinois State University provides plenty to keep a visitor busy. Stop at the university art galleries, the Funk Gem and Mineral Museum, the planetarium, the Hudelson Museum of Agriculture, or the school's historical museum. The Adlai E. Stevenson Memorial Room honors one of Bloomington's most famous citizens. And there really is an academic ivory tower here—Watterson Towers, at twenty-eight stories the world's largest college residence hall. Most campus attractions are free, and tours can be arranged. Call (309) 438–2111 for ISU information. Regular performing arts events are scheduled at Braden Auditorium; call (309) 438–5444.

Illinois Wesleyan, too, boasts a number of treasures including Evelyn Chapel, a focal point of the private school. The chapel is an example of Moravian-style architecture in Flemish patterned brick. The interior woodwork and acoustics are superb. Sheean Library holds the Indian pottery collection of Maj. John Wesley Powell, a former faculty member and first explorer of the Colorado River and Grand Canyon. Call (309) 556–3034 for campus information. McPherson Theater has a busy schedule of productions throughout the year; (309) 556–3232.

Bloomington's **Miller Park Zoo,** 1020 S. Morris Avenue, is one of Illinois's best. The ◆ **Tropical Rain Forest,** 80 feet in diameter, has overhead skylights, a profusion of tropical plants, and colorful exotic birds flying free through the exhibit. Outside, the antics of the California sea lions or the American river otters captivate crowds. The **James E. Gardner Memorial Children's Zoo** features farmyard animals for kids to pet. The zoo is open every day of the year, in the summer 10:00 A.M. to 6:00 P.M. and the rest of the year 10:00 A.M. to 5:00 P.M. Admission: adults $1.50; children 3 to 15 and seniors $1.00. Call (309) 823–4250.

A major seasonal event is Bloomington's **American Passion Play.** Since 1924 community players have enacted the life of Christ in an annual spring tradition with a cast of 350. Sundays, mid-March to early May at the Scottish Rite Temple, 110 E. Mulberry Street; (309) 829–3903.

At 901 N. McLean in Bloomington is the site of the ◆ **Adlai E. Stevenson I home.** Stevenson was vice-president of the United States from 1893 to 1897. Both he and his grandson Adlai Stevenson II, former governor of Illinois, are buried at Evergreen Cemetery here. Another Illinois governor—this one a Republican—also lived in Bloomington. Joseph W. Fifer, governor of Illinois from 1889 to 1893, lived at 909 N. McLean, near the Stevensons. Both homes are privately owned and not open for tours.

Southwest of the county's two major cities is historic **Funks Grove.** One of the county's first settlements, several of the original buildings still remain—the Funk Prairie Home, the 1865 Funk's Grove Church, and the syrup factory. Here, 1,200 gallons per year of maple syrup are produced by the same family that first settled here in 1824. Nearby, stop at the **Lafayette Funk Rock Museum.** To reach Funks Grove take I-55 south to the Shirley exit; the town is about 10 miles southwest of Bloomington. Call (309) 874–3360 for information on the early spring maple tapping, or you can just take home a souvenir bottle or two.

Five miles west of Bloomington on County Road 1650 North, **The Apple Barn** sells tasty bakery products, jams, cider, and fruit from McLean County's oldest commercial orchard. Open daily July through early December; (309) 963–5557.

In Lexington, northeast of the major cities, stands the **Patton Cabin,** built in 1829 by John Patton, one of the county's first white settlers.

91

For campers **Moraine View State Park,** near rural LeRoy, offers 1,700 acres of rolling terrain plus the 160-acre Dawson Lake. Boating, fishing, camping (142 sites, most with electrical hookup), and hiking are popular activities. Call (309) 724–8032.

The center of this county, situated at the center of the state, is **Lake Clinton,** a 5,000-acre cooling lake for the Illinois Power Company's nuclear power plant. With 130 miles of wooded shoreline, the lake development is managed by the Illinois Department of Conservation, which has thoughtfully stocked it with largemouth and smallmouth bass, walleye, crappie, and catfish. Sailboats share the lake with fishing boats, which stop for supplies at Dockside Marina, off Route 10, about 8 miles east of Clinton; (217) 736–2217. In season, hunting is allowed on the land surrounding the lake.

Three miles southeast of Clinton is **Weldon Springs State Recreation Area,** just east of U.S. Highway 51. Prior to 1936 the park was privately owned and the site of a well-known chautauqua each summer. From 1901 to 1920 programs of educational, cultural, or religious interest were presented. By 1904 the yearly event drew so many people that it was necessary to build an auditorium accommodating 4,500 people. They came to hear the stars of the day—William Jennings Bryan, President William Howard Taft, Helen Keller, evangelist Billy Sunday, and temperance leader Carry Nation, among others. The park is open year-round and offers campsites (electric hookups, toilets), picnicking area, hiking trails, fishing, and boating. Weldon Springs has a special handicapped-accessible fishing dock, as well.

The ◆ **DeWitt County Museum** is located in the **Homestead** in Clinton, a restored Victorian mansion listed in the National Register of Historic Places. The 1867 Italianate residence was home to Clinton H. Moore, a former law partner of Abraham Lincoln. The architectural highlight of the structure is a two-story library with vaulted ceiling and iron railing around the open upper gallery. Children will love the antique doll collection and the child's room with its child-sized four-poster bed. Period rooms, a carriage collection, and the farm and railroad museum are among the exhibits. On the last weekend in September the museum sponsors an **Apple and Pork Festival,** featuring stick-to-the-ribs home cooking with plenty of smoked ham and apple cider. During the Christmas season the house is beautifully decorated in the style of the late 1800s. Candlelight tours are also available in December. The museum is open April through December Tuesday through Saturday 10:00 A.M. to 5:00 P.M. and Sunday 1:00 to 5:00 P.M., $2.00 admission. At 219 E. Woodlawn; (217) 935–6066.

A **statue of Lincoln** at the square commemorates the speech delivered in Clinton in 1848 in which Lincoln remarked, "You can fool some of the people all of the time, and all of the people some of the time, but you can't fool all the people all of the time."

Decatur has a cornucopia of architectural styles popular from the Civil War to the Great Depression. Eighty acres of its buildings are listed in the National Register of Historic Places. In addition, the Historic and Architectural Sites Commission has published five walking tours, which take you past examples of Italianate, Second Empire, Queen Anne, Romanesque Revival, Shingle, Stick, Georgian Revival, Tudor, art deco, and neoclassical styles. The walking tours are free and can be obtained from the Decatur Area Convention and Visitors Bureau, 202 E. North Street, Decatur 62523; (217) 423–7000.

Highlights of the tours include the **Milliken Homestead** at 125 N. Pine, a Victorian mansion with fine woodwork, leaded glass, and elegant fireplaces. The **Oglesby Mansion,** 421 W. Williams, is an Italianate-style building with diamond-shaped glass in its bay windows. It was the home of the former United States senator and three-time governor of Illinois, Richard J. Oglesby.

Abraham Lincoln was no stranger to Decatur. It was here at the 1860 Republican Party Convention that he was unanimously nominated for president and also dubbed the "Railsplitter." A **statue of the barefoot Lincoln** stands in Lincoln Square in the center of downtown.

The ✦ **Scovill Children's Zoo** is a special treat because it is designed to look as if the animals and visitors are in the same environment. The zoo encompasses ten acres and lies above the east shore of Lake Decatur. It is open 10:00 A.M. to 6:30 P.M. in the summer and on weekends, May through Labor Day, and 10:00 A.M. to 4:00 P.M. when school is in session. The zoo features rides on the ZO&O Express and admission is $2.00 for adults, $1.50 for children, and $1.25 for seniors. Tours are available by advance arrangement.

To get to Scovill Zoo, take U.S. Highway 36 east and cross Lake Decatur to 71 S. Country Club Road. For information call (217) 421–7435.

The Homestead

The **Macon County Museum Complex,** 5580 N. Fork Road, prides itself on preserving and presenting the heritage of Macon County. The museum has a collection of historic artifacts as well as examples of 1890s houses, a prairie village, and an 1860s schoolhouse. A "hands-on" approach is used in the displays so you can see, smell, and touch the past as well as the present. Museum hours are Tuesday through Sunday 1:00 to 4:00 P.M.; (217) 422–4919.

The ◆ **Mari-Mann Herb Farm and Gingerbread House** is at the north end of St. Louis Bridge Road. Visitors can walk among the herb beds, wildflower fields, deer trails, and formal gardens. The Gingerbread House offers herb products, Special Spoon Herbal Sauce, herbal jellies, and other herbal condiments. Teas, herbs, gourmet spices, fragrances with potpourri, and essential and fragrant oils are also sold.

The herb greenhouse carries a selection of year-round herbal plants.

The farm is open 9:00 A.M. to 5:00 P.M. Monday through Saturday and noon to 5:00 P.M. Sunday. Demonstrations, luncheons, teas, tours, and classes are available by appointment. Contact Mari-Mann Herb Company, Inc., R.R. 4, P.O. Box 7, Decatur 62521; (217) 429–1404.

Decatur is also the home of the **Central Illinois Jazz Festival,** which attracts thousands of jazz musicians and enthusiasts from across the nation. For information call the Holiday Inn, (217) 422–8800.

Western Illinois

1. John Wood Mansion
2. Quincy Museum
3. Villa Katherine
4. Quincy Art Center
5. All Wars Museum
6. Lewis M. Grigsby, Sr., Home
7. Purple Martin Junction
8. Scripps Park
9. Nauvoo Restoration Visitor
   Center
10. Monument to Women
11. Nauvoo State Park
12. Sandburg's birthplace
13. Carl Sandburg Park
14. Galesburg Railroad Museum
15. Knox College
16. Monmouth College

17. Dickson Mound
18. Spoon River Scenic Drive
19. Illinois River Wildlife and
    Fish Refuge
20. Jack Wolf Memorial Fish
    Hatchery
21. New Salem Village
22. Edgar Lee Masters Memorial
    Home
23. George L. Luthy Botanical
    Gardens
24. Lakeview Museum of Arts and
    Sciences
25. McAdams Peak
26. Village of Elsah
27. Annie Louise Keller Memorial

WESTERN ILLINOIS

RIVER TOWNS

The most impressive feature of Quincy, a river town on the east bank of the Mississippi River, is its architecture. Stately mansions and fine old commercial buildings of Italianate, Greek Revival, Romanesque, Queen Anne, Prairie, and Moorish designs fill the town.

The ✦**John Wood Mansion,** 425 S. Twelfth Street, is an example of Greek Revival architecture. The home was built in 1835 by John Wood, founder of Quincy and a former governor of Illinois. Take an escorted tour of the restored home and see the audiovisual presentation. The **Osage Orangerie Gift Shop** is on the premises and offers handcrafted items reminiscent of the early nineteenth century.

The fourteen-room mansion is listed in the National Register of Historic Places. It was originally located across Twelfth Street, but Wood had the house moved to its present site in 1864.

On display are furnishings and many personal items of the Wood family as well as objects recalling Adams County's history. Included are a Victorian dollhouse, the first piano in Quincy, Quincy-made stoves, a table used by Abraham Lincoln, a chandelier from a Mississippi River steamboat, and a sunstone from the Mormon Temple in Nauvoo.

Museum hours are 1:00 to 4:00 P.M. Saturday and Sunday. Other times by appointment. Admission is $2.00 for adults, $1.00 for students; (217) 222–1835.

The ✦ **Quincy Museum** is housed in the Newcomb Stillwell Mansion. The mansion, built in 1891, is listed in the National Register of Historic Places. The exterior has leafy carved ornamentation and window transom bars of solid stone. Building materials of contrasting colors and textures enhance its bold facade and forceful design. It is an example of American architectural style of the 1800s.

The museum exhibits a collection of Indian relics, clothing, weapons, and accessories. There are also African safari trophies and a large collection of fossils, seashells, and butterflies.

In the special discovery area, children can touch museum objects and learn through observation and creative activities. A miniature circus for children, the work of the late Milton Kalmer of Quincy, contains virtually every element of an old-fashioned circus—tiny circus animals, clowns, acrobats, a train, a band with musical instruments, and circus-goers in the stands.

The museum is located at 1601 Maine Street, Quincy 62301; (217) 224–7669. Hours are Tuesday through Sunday 1:00 to 5:00 P.M. Guided tours are available. Admission is $2.00 for adults, $1.00 for students, and free for children under 5.

The ◆ **Villa Katherine,** 532 Gardner Expressway, (217) 223–1000, is a Moorish-style castle. It is located on a bluff overlooking the Mississippi River and is listed in the National Register of Historic Places. The visitors center is open daily 9:00 A.M. to 5:00 P.M. Admission is $1.00 for adults, 50 cents for children. A self-guided tour is also available for $1.00.

The ◆ **Quincy Art Center** is located on the grounds of the Lorenzo Bull Home, 1515 Jersey Street, and is open to the public. The Carriage House was designed by Joseph Lyman Silsbee, a prominent Chicago architect and mentor of Frank Lloyd Wright. The center contains a permanent collection of paintings, sculpture, and graphics, and a library of art books and periodicals. It also has temporary and traveling exhibits. Hours are 1:00 to 4:00 P.M. Tuesday through Sunday. Admission is $1.00 for adults and 50 cents for seniors and students. Phone (217) 223–5900.

Quincy has a number of other museums that are worth visiting. The **Quinsippi Island Antique Auto Museum** is located in Quincy's All-American Park on the banks of the Mississippi River. Sixty-five antique cars and related displays make up the exhibit. The museum's collection includes a 1917 Chevrolet Royal Mail Roadster, a 1911 Little, a St. Louis–built Diana, a 1901 Columbia Electric, a Ford Roadster pickup featured in television's "Hee Haw," and a horse-drawn hearse.

The museum is located at Front and Cedar Streets; (217) 223–4846. Hours are 11:00 A.M. to 5:00 P.M. Sunday and by appointment. Admission is $1.00 for adults, 12 and under 50 cents. The group rate is 75 cents.

The **Gardner Museum of Architecture and Design** is in the Old Public Library Building built in 1888. At Fourth and Maine Streets, it is open from 1:00 to 5:00 P.M. Tuesday through Sunday. The museum contains stained-glass windows from Quincy churches, photographs, and examples of terra-cotta, metal, fine woodwork, and other ornamentation from early Quincy homes. Admission is $2.00 for adults, $1.00 for seniors, and 50 cents for students; (217) 224–6873.

❖ **All Wars Museum,** 1701 N. Twelfth Street, (217) 222–8641, displays military memorabilia with a military library and films. It is on the grounds of the Illinois Veterans Home, one of the nation's largest. Tours are by appointment only; admission is free.

The **Pharmacy Museum of Quincy and Adams County** is located at Fifth and Chestnut Streets. This century-old former drugstore has pharmaceutical artifacts and apothecary items. It also displays antique soft-drink trays, postcards, and an Edison Victrola playing vintage music. Hours are 1:00 to 4:00 P.M. Saturday and Sunday or by appointment. Admission is $2.00 for adults, $1.00 for seniors, and 50 cents for students. Phone (217) 224–1000.

The **Lincoln-Douglas Valentine Museum,** 101 N. Fourth Street, (217) 224–3355, has a unique collection of old and unusual valentines on exhibit. It is open 10:00 A.M. to 2:00 P.M. Monday through Friday. Admission is free.

Quincy's public square at the center of the uptown historical district was originally called John's Square, honoring the United States president for whom both Adams County and Quincy were named. The square became **Washington Square** in 1857. One year later it was the site of the sixth senatorial debate between Lincoln and Douglas. The spot is marked by a commemorative plaque sculpted by Lorado Taft in 1935.

The **Clat Adams General Store** at 200 Front Street was once a favorite haunt of river men, and it is still open to the public. The **Quincy Levee** has steamboats for moonlight excursions and runs daily trips to Hannibal, Missouri, in the summer. Several warehouses and buildings along the levee are from the steamboat era.

Riverview Park on the northeast corner of Quincy, overlooking the Mississippi River, has a statue of George Rogers Clark. This was the site of the Black Hawk War skirmish in Quincy. In **Woodland Cemetery,** South Fifth Street, is a Soldier's Monument dedicated to Adams County men killed in the Civil War, along with the grave of John Wood.

Quincy celebrates its **Annual Dogwood Festival** the first week in May. Festivities include a parade, crafts fair, and military band concert along with the sight of all the dogwood trees in bloom. For a list of events and times, contact the Quincy Chamber of Commerce at (217) 222–7980.

Pittsfield, the county seat of Pike County, was a genuine transplant of New England culture when it was founded in 1833. The settlers came from Pittsfield, Massachusetts, and purchased the site from the federal government for $200.

Pork packing became the chief local industry, and Pittsfield now has the distinction of being the "Pork Capital of the World," with 400,000 to 500,000 hogs marketed there annually. Pittsfield and Pike County residents celebrate **Pig Days** with a day of activities and pork sandwiches and a pork chop dinner. The festival is held during the summer, and the Chamber of Commerce is happy to supply information. Write the chamber at P.O. Box 283, Pittsfield 62363, or call (217) 285–2971.

Pittsfield also has a **Fall Festival** in September that signals the beginning of the harvest season. Again, the Chamber of Commerce has information.

One of the sights to see in Pittsfield is the **home of John Nicolay,** Abraham Lincoln's private secretary. The home is now owned by a private citizen but can be viewed from the street. Nicolay collaborated with John Hay, a personal friend of Lincoln's, in writing a biography of the president. The house is at 500 W. Washington Street.

The home of town philanthropist William Ross no longer stands, but a marker designates the site near the city limits. Ross's mansion was destroyed by fire in 1896. Abraham Lincoln was an overnight guest here when he debated with Stephen A. Douglas in Pittsfield in 1858.

The ◆ **Lewis M. Grigsby, Sr., Home,** 830 E. Washington Street, was built by Colonel Ross's daughter, Mrs. Earl Grigsby, and her friend Mrs. F. M. Lewis, Sr., in 1930. Six generations of the Ross family have resided in Pittsfield, and four generations have lived in this house.

The historic **East School** has recently been restored and is listed in the National Register of Historic Places. The building, built in 1966, is now a museum and a John Wood Community College Learning Center. The building was designed by architect John M. Van Osdel, the "grandfather of Illinois architecture," and includes a renovated clock tower. This building is one of two remaining examples of Osdel's work.

The local community theater group, the **Pittsfield Theatre Guild,** presents five productions a year and is based in the school building. The Chamber of Commerce has information.

101

There is no record of Abraham Lincoln having served in the **Pike County Courthouse,** but nearly 500 documents of cases associated with Lincoln were found in the courthouse. The courthouse is open Monday through Friday 8:00 A.M. to 4:00 P.M.

Just south of Pittsfield, near the village of Time, is the **Pennock Family Farm,** a working sheep ranch. The family puts up a variety of lamb products for direct-mail sales and gift boxes at Christmas time. It's especially pretty in the fall. Call in advance for a visit, (217) 285–2347, or write R.R. 2, Box 214, Pittsfield 62363.

Griggsville is the "Purple Martin Capital of the World." These purple birds are the largest of the swallows, which feed only on flying insects, thus cleaning the air of millions of insects every day.

◆ **Purple Martin Junction** is a ten-acre complex on Route 107 at the south end of Griggsville. A factory that makes aluminum martin houses and an experimental martin colony are on the grounds as is Nature House, a museum. The museum is open Monday through Saturday 10:00 A.M. to 5:00 P.M. and Sunday 1:00 P.M. to 5:00 P.M. Admission is free. The best time to view the martins at Purple Martin Junction is from May to July. For information call (217) 833–2393.

Griggsville may seem an unusual spot for a spice factory, but owner Wayne Riley got his start raising cattle and hogs and found that a tasty mix of seasonings did wonders for a roast. He bottles about six tons of his secret recipe when he isn't preparing hog roasts throughout the Midwest. Contact Riley's Seasoning and Spices, R.R. 2, Box 17, Griggsville 62340; (217) 833–2207.

Pine Lakes Camping and Fishing Resort, 1½ miles north of U.S. Highway 36 near Pittsfield, has camping facilities that include water and electric hookups, laundromat, camp store, recreation room, paddleboat rental, rowboats, bathhouse, and snack bar. Enjoy swimming with attendants on duty, fishing in a forty-five acre lake, horseshoe pits, hayrides, and a playground.

Besides campgrounds, six two-bedroom cottages are available for rent. Contact Pine Lakes Resort, R.R. 3, Box 130A, Pittsfield 62363; (217) 285–6719.

Pike County has its share of natural beauty. Bound by the Mississippi River on the west and the Illinois River on the east, it has rolling countryside and majestic bluffs. Streams, ponds, and small lakes abound for fishing, boating, and swimming. Hunting and camping are also plentiful.

The town of Barry's business district is a turn-of-the-century architectural delight due to a fire in 1894 that caused the town to be rebuilt. The Barry Museum, established in 1984, is housed in the local library and is open year-round by appointment only; (217) 335–2149.

Now a trading center for coal mining and a grain- and fruit-growing region, Rushville began as a tiny wilderness village of twelve families in 1825. It was named for a famous Philadelphia surgeon, Dr. Benjamin Rush. It has stayed a small town with only 3,348 residents.

The community is rich in nineteenth-century history. During the Black Hawk War, Abraham Lincoln and his troops camped near Rushville. It is believed that in 1844 Governor Ford left Springfield with a company of militia and camped overnight in the town square. A tablet in the center of the town square reads, ABRAHAM LINCOLN ADDRESSED THE PEOPLE OF RUSHVILLE ON OCTOBER 20TH, 1858. Lincoln also practiced law in the county courthouse that once stood on this spot.

When Stephen A. Douglas came to Rushville to speak in the senatorial campaign of 1858, his followers arranged a welcome that would be remembered in the town's history. They borrowed a cannon from the nearby community of Beardston, brought it over to the town square, and loaded it with a heavy charge of powder and wet scraps of leather. When the salute to Douglas was fired, the cannon was blown into pieces, miraculously hurting no one.

The **Schuyler County Courthouse** dates back to 1881. It is a two-story building of faded brick and topped with a square clock tower. The cornerstone is dated according to the Masonic calendar and reads JUNE 24 A.L. 5881. The first county building was a log cabin on the north side of the square. In 1829 it was replaced by a plain unornamented brick building, which served until the present courthouse was built on the corner of Lafayette and Congress Streets.

The **Schuyler-Brown County Historical Society** at 200 S. Congress (on U.S. Highway 24, just a block from the courthouse corner) displays genealogical materials and the history of Schuyler and Brown Counties. The center of the building is an old jailhouse. A collection of undertakers' sticks, used to measure the deceased for custom-built coffins, is on display. The society's museum is open daily 1:00 to 5:00 P.M. March through November, and on Sundays the rest of the year.

At the same location is the **Jail Museum,** open daily 1:00 to 5:00 P.M. April 1 to November 1. Winter hours are Saturday and Sunday 1:00 to 5:00 P.M. Admission is free. The museum is open at other times by appointment only. Special exhibits change monthly. Call (217) 322–6975 for more information about these museums.

Tasty souvenirs are to be found at **Bartlow Brothers Meats,** (217) 322–3365. The retail store next to the plant sells heavenly honey-cured hams, bacon, sausages, and a local specialty, Korn Top Wieners.

◆ **Scripps Park** was formerly the eighty-acre farm of Edward Wyllis Scripps, founder of the Scripps-Howard newspaper chain. The park was given to the town in 1922 by Scripps and his two sisters, Virginia and Ellen Browning Scripps. The latter contributed the $100,000 **Community House** that marks the site of the Scripps homestead, the birthplace of Edward Wyllis Scripps. The park is located outside of Rushville, southwest of the junction of U.S. Highway 67 and U.S. Highway 24; (217) 322–3028.

Founded in 1899, **Western Illinois University,** 900 W. Adams, is an important landmark in Macomb and throughout the western part of the state; (309) 295–1414. Over 13,000 students attend the institution.

On campus is the **Western Museum,** on the third floor of Sherman Hall. Its collections feature Civil War memorabilia, American Indian costumes, antique farm implements, and historical materials from the region. Open by appointment only; (309) 298–1727. Free.

If you've got a green thumb, or need to develop one, you'll enjoy the **WIU Greenhouse** at 316 Wagner Hall on campus; (309) 298–1004. The 4,500-square-foot space houses an international collection used in classroom analysis.

The **university library** is known for its unusual pinwheel floor design and a six-story atrium with exhibits and displays throughout. Housing more than 60,000 volumes, it ranks among the top ten largest libraries in the country for nondoctoral degree-granting universities.

On the square in downtown Macomb, the stately **old brick courthouse** is worth a visit, too. Built in the summer of 1872 at a cost of $155,370, the recently renovated building still serves as the center of government. For that matter, there's plenty of history in Macomb. To begin with, the city, founded in 1830, is itself named after Gen. Alexander Macomb, a hero of the War of 1812.

The **Clarence Watson/Wiley Schoolhouse Museum,** 301 W. Calhoun, is a restored 1877 one-room schoolhouse, evocative of the days of pigtails and inkwells. Open 8:30 A.M. to 4:30 P.M. Monday through Friday. It's on the grounds of the United Way. Call (309) 837–9180.

Home of the McDonough County Preservation Society is the **Old Bailey House,** an 1887 Eastlake-style residence at 100 S. Campbell, built by the founder of Macomb's Union National Bank.

The nation's leading manufacturer of art pottery and floral containers is based in Macomb. **Haeger Potteries,** 411 W. Calhoun, has a showroom where you can buy some of the plant's lovely creations. It is open Monday through Saturday 9:00 A.M. to 5:00 P.M. and Sunday 10:00 A.M. to 5:00 P.M.; (309) 833–2171.

Theatergoers have various options. The **Pat Crane Memorial Playhouse** is a popular community theater, with productions running from September through May. Call (309) 837–1828 for ticket information. The playhouse is on St. Francis Road, 2 miles south of Macomb. Western Illinois University has its own **Summer Music Theater** at Brown Hall; (309) 298–1543.

Argyle Lake State Park, 7 miles west of Macomb and 2 miles north of Colchester off U.S. Highway 136, has 1,148 acres of recreational land within its boundaries, including the ninety-five acre Argyle Lake. Interestingly, the State Department of Conservation in 1970 showed a remarkable sense of doing a job right when, after twenty years of bad fishing, the department simply drained the whole lake, removed undesirable species, and restocked the lake with the fish the department wanted. The park takes its name from a group of early settlers of Scottish descent, who called the area Argyle Hollow. The old Galena-to-Beardstown stagecoach passed through here in the early 1800s. Today the park offers visitors picnicking, boating, fishing (for bluegill, largemouth bass, crappie, and channel catfish), camping (electrical outlets available), hiking, and a summer interpretive program. Boats and canoes can be rented. The park is open year-round, and winter brings cross-country skiing, snowmobiling trails, ice skating, and sledding. For more information contact the Site Superintendent, R.R. 2, Colchester 62326; (309) 776–3422.

Hancock County, at the western edge of the state where the Mississippi turns and bends its way around Illinois's bulging middle, has a rich and colorful history inextricably linked with the Mormon religion. It was here, at Nauvoo and Carthage, that

105

some of the most significant—and tragic—chapters of Mormon history were written.

What was once the site of Sauk and Fox Indian villages, by the 1830s had come to be a sleepy river village known as Commerce. After being driven out of Missouri in the spring of 1839, church founder Joseph Smith brought his followers here, to the place he called Nauvoo, to create a homeland for his people. By special negotiation with the Illinois Legislature, the group obtained a charter that allowed its members extraordinary powers—their own courts, militia, university—and any other authority not prohibited by the United States or Illinois constitutions. Nauvoo became virtually an autonomous state. With Mormon converts arriving from across the country and from overseas, the town grew to be Illinois's largest, with 8,000 homes and a population of 15,000 by 1842.

Discontent with the leaders' power grew within and outside of the church. When a group of dissidents published an anti-establishment newspaper with views critical of the leadership, the paper was destroyed. For that, Joseph Smith and his brother, Hyrum, were jailed at the county seat, Carthage. An anti-Mormon mob stormed the jail and murdered the churchmen. Brigham Young took control of the group and led it west to Utah in 1846.

Nauvoo was abandoned until 1849, when a group of French communalists, the Icarians, arrived from Texas to practice their own brand of philosophy under their leader, Etienne Cabet. Their experiment lasted until 1856. During their tenancy, however, they began the production of wine and cheese.

Today groups associated with branches of the Mormon church have extensively restored Nauvoo and the old Carthage jail. The ◆ **Nauvoo Restoration Visitor Center** at Young and Main Streets includes a historical exhibit and a short film on the early days of the community. Admission is free. Call for hours (217) 453–2237. Just outside the center is a sculpture garden, the ◆ **Monument to Women.**

Some of the historic homes and shops open to visit in Nauvoo are the Brigham Young Home; the Mormon newspaper office of the *Times and Seasons*; the Joseph Smith Mansion; Jonathan Browning's gunsmith shop; and the Clark store. Many have guides and period craft demonstrations. The historic homes are open from 9:00 A.M. to 6:00 P.M. in the summer and from 9:00 A.M. to 5:00 P.M. in the winter. Visit around mid-August and enjoy the annual **City of Joseph Smith Pageant**—an outdoor musical event, handsomely costumed and well performed.

Also in Nauvoo be sure to visit the **Joseph Smith Historic Center,** on Water Street off Route 96. Here there is a film, a history of the town, and a walking tour to the log cabin homestead where Smith first lived and the family cemetery.

On the hill overlooking the river plain where the temple community grew are the ruins of Smith's **Great Temple.** The Nauvoo Chamber of Commerce Tourist Reception Center, on Route 96 in the center of town, has a self-guided cassette tape tour and maps of the area available. Open daily 9:00 A.M. to 4:30 P.M. April through October; (217) 453–6648.

Nearby, the ◆ **Nauvoo State Park** features a museum operated by the Nauvoo Historical Society. Camping, a playground, a picnic area, and a stocked fishing lake are also available at the park. For more information contact the Site Superintendent, Nauvoo State Park, P.O. Box 337, Nauvoo 62354; (217) 453–2512.

Labor Day weekend marks the annual **Nauvoo Grape Festival,** (217) 453–6600, with tastings of the local blue cheese and wine, some of the area's best souvenirs. Stop by **Baxter's Winery** on East Parley Street, (217) 453–2528, for tours and tastings. It's recently been reopened by members of the family who've owned the historic winery since the 1800s. Throughout the year, some delightful tastes come from the kitchen of the **Hotel Nauvoo.** The hotel, once a private home, dates from the Mormon period around 1840. In addition to the restaurant, where dinner prices range from $7.00 to $14.00, there are a limited number of overnight accommodations; a double costs $47.50 and up. At 1290 Mulholland; (217) 453–2211.

In Carthage the old jail, which once held Joseph and Hyrum Smith, is at 307 Walnut Street.

Also of interest is the **Hancock County Courthouse,** a Greek Revival structure that's one of the prettiest in the state. It was here, on October 2, 1858, that Abraham Lincoln addressed a crowd of 6,000 in his senatorial campaign against Stephen A. Douglas. A stone marker commemorates the event.

The **Kibbe-Hancock Museum,** across from the old jail on Walnut Street, is the personal collection of former biology professor at the now-closed Carthage College. In addition, area residents have contributed their treasures. The collection includes Civil War relics, World War II memorabilia, Indian artifacts, fossils and rocks, and a natural history exhibit. Free. Call (217) 357–3119 for hours.

Along the western edge of the county, the **Great River Road** runs next to the Mississippi, providing dramatic views and scenic photographic opportunities. In the winter months, from early November through early March, bald eagles roost in the vicinity. January is the best time for observation around the open waters below Lock and Dam No. 19 near Hamilton. From sunrise to around 10:00 A.M. is the best time to catch the eagles feeding. The **Alice Kibbe Life Science Field Station** of Western Illinois University on the Hamilton-Warsaw Road is open for nature observation and hiking at most times of the year. Hank Courtois, resident manager of the station, is available by appointment from 8:00 A.M. to 5:00 P.M. to explain the eagle's natural environment. Call (217) 256–4519.

CARL SANDBURG COUNTRY

Galesburg is a city that retains the flavor of the nineteenth century through its architecture. The city is so proud of its treasures that it has published six walking tours, thirty to forty-five minutes each, that take you through the historic districts, pointing out buildings and telling tales of Galesburg's history. Walking tours are available through the Illinois Department of Tourism or from the Galesburg Area Convention and Visitors Bureau, 154 E. Simmons Street; (309) 343–1194.

In the mid-1830s George Washington Gale, Galesburg's founding father, came to the area to create a labor collective similar to the Oneida Institute of Science and Industry, a collective he founded in New York. Galesburg began as a religious colony under Gale's leadership, and in June 1836, 560 acres were allocated for the town and 104 acres for a college. By the end of the first year, forty families were established in Galesburg.

Railroads were the mainstay of the town. In 1854 the first train, called Reindeer, came to Galesburg. The railroads allowed for area produce to be shipped to other markets and employed a major portion of the town's workforce. By 1880 the town had quadrupled in size and had grown in prosperity as evidenced by the many large Victorian homes here.

Galesburg's public square was the starting point for commerce in the town. The first general store was established at the northwest corner of Broad and Main Streets. The square was traversed by trolley tracks and was proposed as the site of the courthouse or post office. But, after 140 years the square still remains an open, grassy area.

Galeburg's most prominent citizen was Carl Sandburg, noted poet, socialist, biographer, historian, minstrel, and lover of humanity. He lived in Galesburg until he was twenty-four years old. **✦ Sandburg's birthplace,** 331 E. Third Street, the second house east of the Chicago, Burlington, and Quincy Railroad tracks, is now a museum. The house is a three-room cottage bought by August Sandburg, Carl's father, in the fall of 1873. A neighboring house is scheduled to open as a visitors center housing Sandburg exhibits and memorabilia. The museum is open June 1 through Labor Day, noon to 4:30 P.M. Tuesday through Sunday. Call to arrange a tour during the rest of the year, (309) 342–9400.

✦ Carl Sandburg Park is located behind the birthplace. Legend says that Sandburg was so taken with the spot's beauty that he requested it be his final resting place.

In 1966 a memorial named **Remembrance Rock,** after Sandburg's only novel, was erected here. The memorial is a large, red granite boulder unearthed during highway construction northeast of Galesburg. It is a glacial remnant and product of the prairie.

Sandburg's ashes were placed beneath Remembrance Rock in 1967. Ten years later his wife, Lilian Paula Sandburg, was buried beside him.

The house is located in the southwest section of Galesburg. Enter Galesburg via the Main Street off I–74 and follow directional signs through the town. For more information or group appointments, call (309) 342–2361. Museum hours are 9:00 A.M.to 5:00 P.M. daily; closed New Year's, Thanksgiving, and Christmas days.

The **✦ Galesburg Railroad Museum** is at South Seminary and Mulberry Streets. The museum houses a Pullman parlor car, locomotive #3006, and caboose #13501 among other railroad memorabilia. The museum was once the Burlington Northern Depot. Tours of the trains are available during Railroad Days.

Galesburg holds an annual national **Stearman Fly-In** every September. Stearmans are the biplane trainers that gave wings to more military pilots than any other aircraft series in the world. The celebration lasts five days with commercial exhibits, mini-air shows, Stearman contests, aerobatic competition, short-field

109

takeoff, flour-bombing, spot landing, and formation flying contests. For information call the Galesburg Area Convention and Visitors Bureau, (309) 343–1194.

Railroad Days is also a yearly event in Galesburg. Railroad memorabilia, a street fair, and a carnival are part of the festivities. There are also tours of Galesburg's historic sites. Railroad Days is always the fourth weekend in June. For more information contact the Galesburg Area Convention and Visitors Bureau, 154 E. Simmons Street, Galesburg 61401, (309) 343–1194.

The Seminary Street Historic Commercial District on Seminary Street in downtown Galesburg is 2 blocks of restored, turn-of-the-century buildings that house specialty shops and restaurants. For information call the Seminary Street Ltd. office at (309) 342–7061.

Another Galesburg annual event is the Heritage Festival in August. A tram tour through the historic district features shops with "ghosts" from the past. Also featured are old-time craft

Carl Sandburg Birthplace

demonstrations, entertainment, and a Civil War battle reenactment. For information call (309) 344–2839.

The Orpheum Theater, 57 S. Kellogg Street, first opened in 1916 as William J. Olson's vision to raise the public's perception of the meaning of the word "theater" to a level never imagined by builders and audiences of theaters then in local operation. Employing the Chicago architectural firm of C. W. & George L. Rapp, whose philosophy was that a theater should be "a shrine to democracy where the wealthy rub elbows with the poor," Olson created a perfect microcosm of nineteenth-century eclectic architecture. The Orpheum was billed as a vaudeville house and hosted such stars as Jack Benny, George Burns, Houdini, and Fanny Brice. Relegated to a movie theater by the late 1970s, the Orpheum was forced to close down in 1982 due to high operating costs. The theater is now renovated and is a not-for-profit community performing arts center. For a schedule of events, call (309) 342–2299.

✦ **Knox College,** Cherry and South Streets, (309) 343–0112, was built in 1857 and has been described as "a monument to the vision of the founding fathers of both the college and city." **Old Main,** the administration building, was restored and stabilized during the 1930s. It is registered as a national landmark and is an example of American Gothic Revival architecture. Old Main is the only building left standing where Lincoln and Douglas debated in 1858. Hours are 8:00 A.M. to 4:00 P.M.

Knox County Scenic Drive through the Spoon River Valley is a self-guided driving tour. The first two weekends in October are a festival with music, flea markets, arts and crafts, exhibits, and good country cooking. For information call the Galesburg Area Convention and Visitors Bureau.

For fans of old TV westerns, the most important sightseeing stop in the county is surely the house in Monmouth in which Wyatt Earp was born on March 19, 1848; 406 S. Third Street. Earp's birthplace is now a small museum with period furniture. Open 1:00 to 4:00 P.M. Sundays, Memorial Day through Labor Day or by appointment; (309) 734–6419. A memorial to Earp stands in **Monmouth Park.** Although he found a final resting place in California, many of his relatives are buried in Monmouth's **Pioneer Cemetery** on East Archer near Fifth Street. In fact a walk around the old cemetery gives you some historical perspective on the town, which was founded in 1831.

A county landmark is ✦ **Monmouth College,** established in

1853 by a group of Scottish Presbyterians who pioneered the settlement of this part of the state. The campus has many attractive brick buildings in the Greek Revival style. The white-framed **Holt House,** at 402 E. First Avenue, is the birthplace of Pi Beta Phi Sorority. Architecture buffs will also enjoy a drive down **East Broadway,** where the homes are memories of a more gracious period. Historic district status for the area is being pursued.

In front of the castlelike 1895 "Richardsonian Romanesque" county courthouse in Monmouth stands a **statue of Gen. Abner C. Harding,** a hero at the second battle of Fort Donaldson during the Civil War.

And though Dixon claims the title as Ronald Reagan's boyhood home, Monmouth, too, shares the honor, for the family lived here briefly during the former president's early years, at 218 S. Seventh Street (now a private residence).

Western Stoneware Company, 521 Sixth Avenue, (309) 734–2161, is the oldest maker of pottery and stoneware in the Midwest. The maple-leaf emblem that appeared on Western Stoneware's jugs and crocks produced here came from Monmouth's epithet as Maple City (especially well-earned in the fall when the city's thousands of maple trees are ablaze with color). Though no factory tours are available, the retail outlet, **The Pottery Barn,** located at U.S. Highway 34 and U.S. Highway 67, is open daily. Hours are 9:30 A.M. to 4:30 P.M. except Sunday, noon to 4:30 P.M.

Each year right after Labor Day, the **Warren County Prime Beef Festival** is held in Monmouth. There are livestock shows, parades, a demolition derby, and a carnival. Call (309) 734–3181 for more information.

For recreation during the warmer months, the eighteen holes of **Gibson Woods Golf Course** are open to the public. The course is adjacent to Monmouth Park on U.S. Highway 34 immediately northeast of Monmouth, (309) 734–9968.

Monmouth Airport, northeast of town on U.S. Highway 34, is the oldest continually operating airport in the state.

Out in the rural part of the county, visit the **County Historical Museum** in Roseville.

If old bones, skulls, and Indian burial grounds grab your interest, Fulton County is the place you should visit. It is one of the richest archaeological areas in the Midwest. There are 800 mounds in Fulton centered at the junction of the Spoon and

Illinois Rivers. The most famous is the ❧ **Dickson Mound** near Lewiston.

The Dickson Mound is on a high bluff overlooking the two rivers. It was originally crescent-shaped with the points facing east. It measures 550 feet along its outer curve and 35 feet high. A reproduction of one of the burials is exhibited at the Field Museum of Natural History in Chicago.

A museum adjacent to the mound has the largest display of its kind in the country, exhibiting more than 200 skeletons. It is one of the few on-site archaeological museums in the Midwest.

The museum's collection includes remains and artifacts displayed in their original position when found, pottery, vessels, mussel-shell spoons, el-shaped pipes, bone needles, beads, stone adze blades, and effigy forms.

A colored-light display highlights the ghostly features of Indian skeletons, and maps and cases explain the Mississippian Indian culture of 1000 B.C.

Down the hill from the museum is a reconstructed village of the same period.

The mound is located off Route 97 and Route 78 near Havana, 5 miles south of Lewiston. Museum hours are 8:30 A.M. to 5:00 P.M. daily and closed on holidays. The gift shop and coffee shop are closed from mid-December to April 1. Grounds are open to dusk from May 1 to November 1. Admission is free; (309) 547–3721.

For the literary-minded, Edgar Lee Masters immortalized the Spoon River Country and particularly Lewiston in his *Spoon River Anthology*. Masters's home was in Lewiston, and **Oak Hill Cemetery** on North Main Street shows many names identical to characters in the anthology. The area is also filled with interesting buildings, historic markers, and antiques shops.

The **Ross Mansion,** 409 E. Milton Avenue, was the inspiration for the McNeely Mansion in the anthology. The mansion was modeled after a home on the Hudson River that Col. Lewis W. Ross admired. The New England–style home has seventeen rooms and is made of stone from the Spoon River Valley.

Maj. Newton Walker's house had the honor of having had Abraham Lincoln as a guest. The home was built in 1833 and is located at 1127 N. Main Street. Unfortunately, it is not open to the public.

Other places of interest in Lewiston are the **Phelps Store,** Main and Washington Streets (originally an Indian trading post), and the **Church of St. James** at Broadway and Illinois Streets, an example of Victorian Gothic architecture.

In the nearby town of Ellisville is an **opera house** from the nineteenth century, and in London Mills is the **Ross Hotel,** an authentically restored hotel.

The ◆ **Spoon River Scenic Drive** takes you through 60 miles of woodland and towns. To obtain a map from the Spoon River Scenic Drive Associates, write to them at Box 59, Ellisville 61431, or call (309) 293–2143. Also, signs mark the drive.

The first two weekends in October are the **Annual Spoon River Festival.** Spoon River Country also has a **Spoon River County Christmas Festival** the first Saturday in December. The festival offers crafts, music, dancing, and food. Contact the Spoon River Scenic Drive Associates for information.

Some of the greatest concentrations of wild ducks and geese in the nation are to be found in the ◆ **Illinois River Wildlife and Fish Refuge** in Mason County. These feathered creatures contribute to the area's reputation as a hunting and fishing paradise.

The refuge is a vital link in the chain of resting, feeding, and wintering areas for migratory birds along the Mississippi Flyway. During the annual migration ducks and geese are often so numerous their masses darken the sky.

The refuge has 4,500 acres of land and water where wild ducks and geese can be observed each fall and winter. The average peak concentration during early winter exceeds 100,000 ducks and up to 40,000 Canada, blue, and snow geese. Mallards make up most of the duck population, with smaller numbers of wood ducks, pintail, widgeon, black duck, blue-winged teal, scaup, shoveler, gadwall, goldeneye, and mergansers.

The wood duck is the most common nester in the refuge. Wood ducks normally rest in natural cavities in hardwood timber, but they have adapted to nesting boxes erected in the refuge.

Bald eagles winter in several concentrated groups here. More than 240 eagles have been counted along the river. Eagles usually arrive in October and stay until the ice disappears in the spring.

More than 275 species of birds reside in the refuge. Great blue herons, green herons, great egrets, and black-crowned night herons are generally summer residents. Marsh, water, and shorebirds are common during the spring and fall, and their migration is spectacular during August and early September.

The refuge is open to the public, and an interpretive foot trail is located in the headquarters. Roads next to portions of the refuge offer opportunities for viewing wildlife without disturbing them. Fishing, mushroom and berry picking, and hiking are permitted. **Lake Chautauqua** is known for its bluegill, crappie, and catfish fishing especially during April, May, and early June.

Waterfowl hunting is permitted in the Liverpool section, located outside Lake Chautauqua.

For additional information contact the Refuge Manager, Illinois River Wildlife and Fish Refuge, R.R. 2, Havana 62644; (309) 535–2290. The refuge is 8 miles northeast of Havana on the Manito blacktop. A sign marks the entrance.

The ❖ **Jack Wolf Memorial Fish Hatchery,** 4 miles west of Manito on Oil Well Road, has 160 acres within the Sand Ridge State Forest. The hatchery is named after the late Jacob John "Jake" Wolf, who was once deputy director of the Department of Conservation for the State of Illinois. Wolf is remembered as a friend of the outdoor sportsman and sportswoman. During Wolf's career as a state legislator and a member of the Department of Conservation, numerous conservation bills were passed that benefited hunting and fishing enthusiasts statewide.

The complex includes a 36,000-square-foot hatchery building, fifty-six indoor rearing tanks, spawning and egg incubation facilities, modern fish harvest, and distribution and feeding systems. Outside are twenty-two acres of solar ponds that use energy from the sun to heat water for fish production, twenty-eight rearing raceways, and seven brood raceways.

Specialties of the hatchery are chinook, coho salmon, rainbow and brown trout, walleye, muskellunge, northern pike, striped bass, bluegill, channel catfish, and large- and smallmouth bass. The fish produced at the hatchery are used to stock Lake Michigan, private farm ponds, state-owned lakes, reservoirs, streams, and rivers. Anticipated production at the hatchery is forty-two million fish a year.

Tours are on a self-guided basis, although employee-guided tours can be scheduled for large groups. Visiting hours are 8:30 A.M. to 3:30 P.M. daily; (309) 968–7531.

If the Midwest were Arabia, then surely ❖ **New Salem Village** would be its Mecca, for thousands of pilgrims journey here each year for a glimpse of the relics of Lincoln. The state park, 2 miles south of the county seat, Petersburg, on Route 97, is a reconstruction of the village in which Lincoln lived from 1831 to 1837. Admission to the park is free.

Here homes, shops, and taverns take you back to the time when Lincoln was just beginning his political career. He served here as postmaster and deputy surveyor and was defeated for election to the Illinois General Assembly in 1832, then elected two years later.

The 1835 **Onstot Cooper Shop** is the only original building on the site, and it was here that Lincoln studied law books late in the night. The **Lincoln-Berry store** is an authentic re-creation of the general store in which Lincoln was a partner. At the **Rutledge Tavern** lived his first love, Ann Rutledge (who is buried in Oakland Cemetery in Petersburg).

Costumed interpreters run the shops and exhibits, so you may encounter a blacksmith at a forge, a baker taking freshly baked bread from the oven, or a candlemaker working with tallow. Oxen and other farm animals are part of the scene. Inside the park flowers and plants have been planted for historic authenticity. Vegetable gardens and herb gardens are tucked behind the cabins and wild plum, blackberry, gooseberry, and other trees and shrubs add to the look of the 1830s village.

The park has camping facilities available on the grounds (178 campsites, showers, and electric hookups available). For more information contact Site Superintendent, R.R. 1, Box 244A, Petersburg 62675; (217) 632–4000.

Take a ride on the **paddlewheel steamboat *Talisman,*** a replica of the only steamboat to successfully navigate the Sangamon River. Forty-five-minute trips begin at the dock just steps away from New Salem Village. The 2½-mile excursion operates daily from May to Labor Day and then on weekends only through October; (217) 632–7681.

In Petersburg at Jackson and Eighth Streets, is the ❖ **Edgar Lee Masters Memorial Home.** The poet and author of *Spoon River Anthology* lived here as a boy. Much of his work reflects the feeling of this part of Illinois. Restored to its 1875 period, the home holds memorabilia of the family and his work. Open Memorial Day through Labor Day daily afternoons only. Admission is free; (217) 632–7363. Masters is buried in the town's **Oakland Cemetery.**

Petersburg is home to a wonderful bed-and-breakfast: **Bit of Country,** 122 W. Sheridan, (217) 632–3771. Bit of Country is in a restored 1868 home with a guest house.

Lincoln Log Cabin

They used to ask, "Will it play in Peoria?" These days it decidedly does. Named one of the country's "All-America" cities in 1989 and called an "in" place to live by *Business Week* magazine, Peoria's a hit.

The ✦ **George L. Luthy Botanical Gardens,** 2218 N. Prospect Road, (309) 686–3362, has a rose garden with more than 800 all-American award-winning selections. The All-Seasons Garden has plants selected for their unique characteristics that provide beauty all year-round. The herb garden has plants that are pleasant to smell and add zest to culinary arts.

The conservatory is the permanent home of a collection of tropical plants and fragile specimens and the bio-center has education programs, workshops, films, and seminars.

Admission to the gardens is free, and they are open from dawn to dusk. The conservatory and gift and plant shop are open 8:00 A.M. to 4:00 P.M. weekdays, 10:00 A.M. to 4:00 P.M. weekends.

The ✦ **Lakeview Museum of Arts and Sciences,** 1125 W.

Lake, (309) 686–7000, has antiques, archaeology, astronomy, geology, folk art, music, wildlife, and movie exhibitions. The main exhibit is "Man and Nature: The Changing Relationship." It is a multimedia program telling the story of humankind's ties with nature from prehistoric to present times.

The Decorative Art Gallery has English, French, and American furniture from the eighteenth to the twentieth centuries. Other collections include fine arts, anthropology, history, and natural sciences.

The Planetarium gives laser light concerts and has a museum shop, sales/rental gallery, and bookstore. For a listing of planetarium shows, call (309) 686–6682.

Museum hours are Tuesday through Saturday 10:00 A.M. to 5:00 P.M., Wednesday evening 7:00 to 9:00 P.M., and Sunday noon to 5:00 P.M. The museum is closed on Mondays and major holidays. Admission to the museum is free; the Planetarium show is $2.25 for adults, $1.25 for students, and $1.00 for children and seniors.

The **Wildlife Prairie Park** began as the project of the Forest Park Foundation. The theme was native North American animals living in natural habitat enclosures, with other areas of the park portraying Illinois's natural history. A 24-inch gauge railroad system travels through the park.

The park offers special events that include the Illinois Art League show, tree-planting parties, and Pops on the Prairie Concerts with the Peoria Symphony Orchestra.

From May through October, hours are 10:00 A.M. to 6:30 P.M. From November to April, weekday hours are 11:00 A.M. to 4:00 P.M.; weekends, 9:00 A.M. to 4:30 P.M. A gift shop and country store are on the grounds.

The park is located 10 miles west of downtown Peoria, off I–74 via exit 82 on Taylor Road. Weekday admission is $3.50 for adults, $1.75 for ages 5 to 17, 4 and under free. Weekend admission is $4.00 for adults, $2.00 for ages 5 to 17, 4 and under free. Call (309) 676–0998.

The **Peoria Historical Society,** 942 N.E. Glen Oak, (309) 674–1921, offers scenic and historic bus tours of Peoria. The tour starts downtown and travels through the Fort Clark site on the Illinois riverbank, the historic courthouse plaza, and city hall. Narrated group tours are available for half a day or a full day and include lunch. For information contact the society.

Two houses that are of interest and available for viewing are the **Flanagan House,** 942 N.E. Glen Oak Avenue, and the **Pettengill-Morton House,** 1212 W. Moss Avenue. Both houses were constructed in the 1800s and are furnished in period style. Call (309) 674–1921 for tours. Admission is $2.00 for adults, 50 cents for children under 12. The houses are open Sunday 2:00 to 4:30 P.M. March through December or by appointment.

PERE MARQUETTE COUNTRY

Father Jacques Marquette, a French Jesuit missionary, and explorer Louis Joliet, were the first Europeans to come to this area in 1673. The history of the area, however, is traceable back some 200 million years when movements of the earth resulted in dislocation of rocks, producing the Lincoln Fold in Pere Marquette State Park.

Pere Marquette State Park lies 5 miles west of Grafton on Route 100 in Jersey County. It is an 8,000-acre park lying on bluffs that overlook the confluence of the Mississippi and Illinois Rivers.

Another trace of prehistoric times is ❖ **McAdams Peak,** where twin springs flow from Ordovician-Silurian rocks that were deposited in the sea 350 million years ago. All the ridges have loess (pronounced *less*) on them. Loess is windblown dust laid down a million years ago during the Great Ice Age. The river's banks of yellow clay are composed of loess and capped with black topsoil that supports the forest.

Prehistoric people also left their mark here. There are eighteen sites indicating their presence, and a village once stood where the park lodge now stands. Nomadic hunters and fishers lived in the Illinois valley about the beginning of the Christian era, and Stone Age people left remnants of arrowheads and coarse, heavy pottery.

When the French came to this region, the tribes of Illinois, Potawatomi, and Kickapoo Indians remained near their ancestral cemeteries and burial mounds. Their houses and village sites dotted the Illinois Valley and are still visible throughout the park.

The **Pere Marquette Lodge,** located in the park, (618) 786–2331, has been remodeled. There are fifty rooms and twenty-two cabins, plus an indoor swimming pool. There is a dining room and a 700-ton stone fireplace in the lobby. The park also has what is believed to be the world's largest chess set. The board is 12 feet square and has figures bigger than the average six-year-old.

119

Within the grounds is an amphitheater with a movie screen. The theater seats about 200 people. There are also facilities for boating, camping, fishing, and picnicking, and more than 15 miles of hiking trails and horseback riding. Watch for American bald eagles in the bluffs throughout the area.

The visitors center displays the history of the park, and a park interpreter is available for assisting bus tours, hikes, demonstrations, and talks to large groups. The visitors center is open 8:30 A.M. to 4:00 P.M. year-round. For reservations with the interpreter, call (618) 786–3323 or write Park Interpreter, Pere Marquette State Park, Box 325, Grafton 62037.

Just downriver away from Grafton is the quaint ◆ **Village of Elsah,** the first entire community to be listed on the National Register of Historic Places. On the Great River Road, this Mississippi River town seems more like a New England village. Plan a stay at the charming **Corner Nest Bed and Breakfast,** 3 Elm Street. The 1883 French-American mansion overlooks the river with a popular screened porch. Each of the four rooms is decorated with antiques. Phone (618) 374–1892 or write P.O. Box 220, Elsah 62028.

Greene county lies in the west-central part of the state on the Illinois River, about 20 miles from its mouth. Primarily an agricultural region, the terrain is marked by broken, hilly land as its western edge along the river bluffs. Here fruit cultivation is an important industry.

A number of historic sites are found throughout the county: In Carrollton, the county seat, the **Hodges Building** on the northwest corner of the town square houses the Greene County Historical Society. The **County Courthouse,** along with the entire square, is listed in the National Register of Historic Places. On the west side of the town square is the former **home of Maj. Marcus Reno,** who fought with Custer in the Battle of Little Big Horn.

The **Henry T. Rainey Home** is one-half mile east of Carrollton on Route 108. The three-story brick house faced with columns holds a wealth of historical artifacts. Rainey was the Speaker of the House in the Seventy-third Congress. In **Rainey Memorial Park,** on the north edge of town, a bronze statue honors the legislator who served in every session except one from 1903 until his death in 1934.

One of the few working farm vacations in the state can be had at **Hobson's Bluffdale Farm,** 4 miles north of Eldred on the Bluff blacktop road. It's good old-fashioned fun with plenty of outdoor activity. The farm holiday includes lodging, truly memorable meals, horseback riding, boating, hayrides, and swimming. The 1828 **John Russell House** is situated on the property, as well. For reservations, call (217) 983–2854.

Other recreational opportunities are available at **Greenfield Lake,** 1½ miles east of Greenfield, and **Roodhouse Reservoir,** 2 miles east of Roodhouse. Both offer camping, fishing, and boating. But, of course, the **Illinois River** is the major body of water in these parts. Try waterskiing downstream or take a free ferry from the terminus of Route 108, west of Eldred, across to Calhoun County.

For golfers there is the **Lone Oak Golf Course,** 3 miles east of Carrollton on Route 108, then right 1¼ miles on the country road. The nine-hole course is situated in a beautiful rural setting; (217) 942–6166.

In Whitehall, which is in the northern part of the county, the ◆ **Annie Louise Keller Memorial** is a sculpture by the famous artist, Lorado Taft, dedicated to a schoolteacher who lost her life rescuing her pupils during a tornado in 1927. Here, too, is the **grave of the Little Drummer Boy of Shiloh.**

Plan a drive along the river bluffs from Eldred to Hillview. It's especially pretty in the fall.

SOUTHEASTERN ILLINOIS

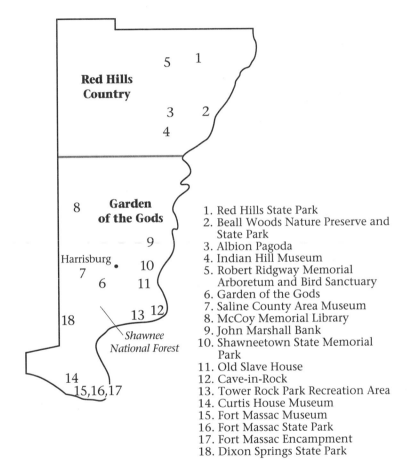

Red Hills Country

5   1

3   2

4

8   **Garden of the Gods**

9

Harrisburg

7   10

6   11

18

13 12

Shawnee National Forest

14

15,16,17

1. Red Hills State Park
2. Beall Woods Nature Preserve and State Park
3. Albion Pagoda
4. Indian Hill Museum
5. Robert Ridgway Memorial Arboretum and Bird Sanctuary
6. Garden of the Gods
7. Saline County Area Museum
8. McCoy Memorial Library
9. John Marshall Bank
10. Shawneetown State Memorial Park
11. Old Slave House
12. Cave-in-Rock
13. Tower Rock Park Recreation Area
14. Curtis House Museum
15. Fort Massac Museum
16. Fort Massac State Park
17. Fort Massac Encampment
18. Dixon Springs State Park

SOUTHEASTERN ILLINOIS

RED HILLS COUNTRY

One mile northeast of Sumner in Lawrence County is ❖ **Red Hills State Park,** a 948-acre park of high wooded hills, deep ravines, meadows, and year-round springs. Hickory, oak, sycamore, maple, gum, crab, walnut, and apple trees grow in abundance in this area. Squirrels, doves, woodcock, quail, and rabbit live and multiply in this haven for nature lovers and sports enthusiasts.

U.S. Highway 50 divides the park into two sections, and the park itself is a historical crossroad, the westernmost edge being the first land in Illinois ceded by the Indians to the United States government. The borderline runs through the park from southwest to northeast and was set by a treaty made in 1795 at Greenville, Ohio, by Gen. Anthony Wayne and the Indians. The Indians relinquished all claims to the land northwest of the Ohio River and east of a specified line. The area was called the Vincennes Tract.

The name Red Hill comes from the peak by the same name, which is the highest point along the Baltimore and Ohio Railroad between Cincinnati and St. Louis. Red Hill is topped by a tower and cross, constructed and financed by residents cooperating in an interdenominational council.

The park has picnicking, fishing, boating, camping, and hunting facilities. A park interpreter conducts summer recreation programs. There is a trail through the woods, and other areas are suitable for hiking. Ice fishing and ice skating are permitted in season. The park is open from sunrise to 11:00 P.M. daily. For more details contact Red Hills State Park, R.R. 4, Sumner 62466; (618) 936–2469.

Lawrence County residents like to celebrate, and there are four festivals of note: **Bridgeport SummerFest,** the last weekend in June; **Sumner Fall Festival,** the first weekend after Labor Day; **St. Francisville Chestnut Festival,** the first weekend in October; and the **Lawrenceville Fall Festival,** the third weekend in September. For exact dates and a list of activities contact the Lawrence County Chamber of Commerce, 1104 Jefferson Street, Lawrenceville 62349; (618) 943–3516.

For real nature buffs ❖ **Beall Woods Nature Preserve and State Park,** 6 miles south of Mount Carmel in Wabash County,

124

is the largest tract of original deciduous forest remaining in the United States and is relatively untouched by human beings. Sixty-four species of trees have been identified in the forest, and there is reason to believe that more will be discovered. Approximately 300 trees with trunks greater than 30 inches in circumference at chest height are in the park.

The tract of land that is now the park was under the ownership of the Beall family for more than 102 years. After the death of Laura Beall, the property was sold to a man who intended to clear the land and farm it. Conservation-minded individuals and groups helped to create the original acquisition by the state of Illinois in 1965 by evoking the law of eminent domain against unwilling settlers in order to preserve the virgin woodland for posterity.

Beall Woods is a registered landmark and is listed as the "Forest of the Wabash." The woods are made up of 270 acres of primeval woodland that borders the Wabash River, and the area was dedicated as an Illinois nature preserve to ensure that the forest will remain in its natural condition.

Beall Woods is sometimes referred to as the "University of the Trees" because it is a living forest community with a natural ecological system containing native plant and animal life. Hikers can view red fox, deer, raccoon, and pileated woodpeckers, and the forest floor supports a variety of interesting flowers.

There are plenty of hiking trails for those interested. The trails begin at the **Red Barn,** a remodeled barn that serves as a nature center. It has a display of seeds, native woods of Illinois, and Indian arrowheads. Hours are 7:00 A.M. to 4:00 P.M. daily.

There are also facilities for picnicking and a playground. The park is open year-round except for Christmas and New Year's Day. For information contact the Site Superintendent, Beall Woods Conservation Area, R.R. 2, Mount Carmel 62863; (618) 298-2442. Beall Woods is near Keensburg off Route 1, about 6 miles south of Mount Carmel.

Edwards County is known as the Chowder Capital of the World. The aroma of this fragrant dish can be detected around the county anytime from June through September.

There is no exact information on when chowder became popular here, but records from the time of the Civil War indicate that it was enjoyed as early as the 1860s.

Chowder is generally cooked in large black kettle cauldrons, ranging in size from twenty to seventy gallons. A variety of ingredients, including tomatoes, are added to boiling water; chowder time traditionally starts when the tomatoes ripen and closes with the heavy frost.

Several communities in Edwards County hold chowder festivals, and the **Edwards County Historical Society,** 212 W. Main Street, Albion 62806, (618) 445–2631, has information on Albion and other communities' chowder festivals.

The ◈ **Albion Pagoda** in Albion was erected in 1914 and is the town's pride. The first pagoda was built around the mineral-water well in 1890. The waters were said to cure rheumatism, kidney and urinary troubles, "derangements of the stomach and bowels," and many other afflictions. When the original pagoda deteriorated, a second one was built in the same location; then in 1906 the current two-story structure replaced the two previous ones. The third pagoda was designed by architect W. E. Felix of Fairfield and constructed as a community program by the Albion Women's Beautifying Club.

The pagoda is octagonal with eight brick columns. The roof is made of red clay, resembling the roofs of the pagodas in East Asia.

Bone Gap is a name that brings images of hunting and Indians to mind. The ◈ **Indian Hill Museum** in Bone Gap has exhibits of pioneer life and woodworking and blacksmith shops from early railroad days. Besides a collection of Indian artifacts, the museum has family heirlooms and historical items pertaining to the English settlements in the Wabash Valley.

Museum founders Norman and Sandy Reid's main objective is to educate the younger generation and create an air of reminiscence for others. You'll find a 1920 Keck-Gonnerman steam engine, which was used to power a sawmill and threshing machine, more than 10,000 Indian artifacts, including some dating back to the Archaic period 10,000 years ago, and a Regina music box with a cherrywood case and hand-painted view of the Midwest that dates to 1861. Norman Reid also has a collection of more than 300 guns, which includes handguns ranging from the Civil War period to the 1880 period, and an ancient buffalo skull that was found on the plains more than 107 years ago.

The museum is open Wednesday through Sunday from 9 A.M. to 5:00 P.M.; (618) 446–3277. Admission is by donation. The museum is on Route 3 in Bone Gap (from Albion take Route 130 to Route 3).

Olney is the home of the white albino squirrel. Local legend says that the white squirrel first appeared here in 1902. A hunter captured two squirrels, a male and a female, and put them on display in a town saloon.

Another townsman heard about the squirrels and sent his son over to get the animals and release them in the woods. As soon as the squirrels were freed, a large fox squirrel jumped down from a tree and killed the male. The son shot the fox squirrel as he tried to attack the female. Weeks later baby white albino squirrels were seen, and the population has increased to about 800 albino squirrels.

A city ordinance has been enacted to protect these special citizens. A white squirrel has the right of way on any street in Olney, and a motorist is fined $25 for running over one. Anyone caught taking one out of town also will be fined.

Olney residents are also protective of their bird population. At Bird Haven in ❖ **Robert Ridgway Memorial Arboretum and Bird Sanctuary,** you can walk and observe nature. Robert Ridgway, a naturalist, scientist, artist, and author is famous for his books *Birds of Middle and North America* and *Color Stands and Color Nomenclature.* He was associated with the Smithsonian Institution and was a zoologist for the Survey of the Fortieth Parallel. He was also an authority in the field of ornithology.

Ridgway purchased the eighteen acres of Bird Haven in 1906. By the 1920s the arboretum and bird sanctuary was said to have had the second-largest number of plant species, second to a larger tract in Japan.

The Ridgway summer cottage once stood on the grounds, and a replica of the front porch has been reproduced on the cottage site. Dr. Ridgway's grave is on the grounds and is marked by a granite boulder with a bronze plaque with birds sculpted on it.

Bird Haven's hours are from dusk to dawn. For more information contact Olney City Hall, 300 Whittle Avenue, Olney 62450; (618) 395–7302. Bird Haven is a half mile northeast of Olney on East Fork Lake Road.

Olney holds an annual **Arts and Crafts Festival** every fall. It is a performing arts showcase open to amateur and professional fine artists and craftspeople. Contact the Olney Arts Council, P.O. Box 291, Olney 62450, for specific dates and entry information.

GARDEN OF THE GODS

In the southeast corner of the county, where it joins Gallatin and Hardin Counties, the ✦ **Garden of the Gods** is one of the state's most dramatic natural attractions. Created more than 200 million years ago from geologic uplifting, spectacular rock outcroppings have been formed through the action of water and wind. The unusual rock formations have been given names by imaginative explorers—Camel Rock, Noah's Ark, Mushroom Rock, Fat Man's Squeeze, and Tower of Babel are some of the more colorful ones.

One mile of well-maintained trails and 5 miles of semideveloped trails allow hikers to trek through the low mountainous region. Part of the Shawnee National Forest, which runs across the width of southern Illinois, the Garden of the Gods is a perfect spot for camping. For information on the Garden of the Gods, contact the Shawnee National Forest Headquarters, (618) 253–7114. Just north is the Saline County Conservation Area with its Glen O. Jones Lake.

Harrisburg, the county seat, was at one time a major center for tobacco growing and, later, coal mining. Here the ✦ **Saline County Area Museum,** 1600 Feazel Street, is a popular attraction. Set in a parklike setting are a handful of furnished historic buildings, moved here from around the area. You can visit an 1800s one-room schoolhouse, an old Moravian church, a log cabin, general store, post office, and barn with its original threshing floor. The museum is open Tuesday through Saturday 9:00 A.M. to 4:00 P.M. and Sunday 1:00 to 4:00 P.M. Admission is $2.00 for adults, $1.00 for children. For information call (618) 253–5085.

The prize of McLeansboro, the Hamilton County seat, is the ✦ **McCoy Memorial Library,** on the west side of the public square. The Cloud Family built this handsome brick Victorian mansion, with a central tower and unique roofline, in 1884. It is listed in the National Register of Historic Places. Along with an 8,000-volume collection, the library boasts countless antiques on display for visitors. A central feature of the home is the number of noteworthy fireplaces throughout the structure. On the second floor, the **Hamilton County Historical Society Museum** exhibits souvenirs of the area's past. Open Monday, Wednesday, and Friday 1:00 to 4:00 P.M. Admission is $1.00 The library is open every day but Sunday.

Next to the library building and once a residence is the **People's National Bank,** built by the same family, the Clouds, and also listed in the National Register.

For a bite of something to eat, the hearty fare at **Pat's City and Country Cafe** on Route 14 East is some of the best in the county. Stop for shopping at **Southfork Antique Mall,** 105 E. Broadway in McLeansboro.

Although today we can get in our cars and speed hundreds of miles over broad, smoothly paved interstate highways, travelers in the first part of the nineteenth century turned to rivers and riverboats for efficient travel. And of those rivers, the Ohio was one of the longest and most frequently chosen routes, an interstate expressway from Pennsylvania all the way to the Mississippi River. Thus, the importance of Gallatin County and its seat, Shawneetown, is clearly understood in terms of a river port. Today one of the world's longest span cantilever bridges crosses the Ohio at Shawneetown.

Shawnee Indians had a village here in the mid-1700s, and burial mounds can be seen throughout the area. The earliest white settlers arrived around 1800. In 1810 the federal government laid out Shawneetown on the river, and it quickly became a major port and gateway for immigrants into the new frontier. In 1814 it became the first incorporated town in Illinois. A ferry service, crossing the river into Kentucky, was begun. Four years later the U.S. Land Office for southeastern Illinois opened at Shawneetown. Adding to the economic growth of the community were the nearby saltworks at Equality, which supplied an important pioneer commodity and shipped salt throughout the region. Thus, Shawneetown became an important financial center in the American westward movement. One early resident was Gen. Thomas Posey, a member of George Washington's staff who was present for the British surrender at Yorktown. He is buried 2 miles north of the town in **Westwood Cemetery.**

The first bank in the territory opened here in 1816. Known as the ◆**John Marshall Bank** for the early merchant who began it in his house, the brick structure has been reconstructed by the local historical society and is open for tours by appointment. There are also walking tours available that take in a number of sites in the historic town.

A second bank, the 1839 **First State Bank,** is a handsome Greek Revival building with Doric columns supporting a portico. (It's now

129

listed in the National Register of Historic Places.) For its construction, sandstone was floated down the Ohio by flatboat from quarries in the East. A favorite local story is of the time when businessmen from the tiny village of Chicago rode to Shawneetown to ask bankers there for a loan. They were refused on the grounds that Chicago was much too far from Shawneetown ever to prosper.

The Ohio River proved a blessing and a curse for the community. Major floods struck the town in 1884, 1898, 1913, and 1937. In 1937 residents rebuilt their community in the hills 3 miles inland. In Old Shawneetown, the original settlement, many of the old landmarks are part of ❖ **Shawneetown State Memorial Park,** on the banks of the river.

The most famous visitor of all to come to Shawneetown was Marquis de Lafayette. The Revolutionary War hero was honored here at a reception at the Rawlings' Hotel on May 7, 1825. Gov. Edward Coles greeted the soldier at the waterfront. The hotel burned in 1904 and was rebuilt.

Equality, at the west side of the county near Route 142 and Route 13, was the site for the United States Salines, salty springs first discovered by the Indians. Later, French and American settlers made salt at the site. As an important early industry, the springs became the property of first the federal, then the state government. Andrew Jackson, before becoming president, attempted to lease these springs. Today only some crumbling foundations remain. A mural in the **Gallatin County Courthouse** depicts these salt-making operations.

Three miles east of Equality, off Route 1 south of the junction of Route 1 and Route 13, is the ❖ **Old Slave House,** a National Historic Landmark and the county's top visitor attraction. This mansion, named Hickory Hill, was erected in 1834 by John Crenshaw, one of the lessees of the government salt springs, who became quite wealthy in that trade. Another trade in which it is suggested he made money was the slave trade, and the third floor of the house holds cells with anchor chains on the floors. Open April through November daily 9:00 A.M. to 5:00 P.M. and through the winter months by appointment only; (618) 276–4410.

At the northwest border of the county, at New Haven, once stood the mill of Jonathan Boone, who was the brother of Daniel Boone. Jonathan Boone died here in 1808. A state historical marker records the spot today.

Ridgway, in the center of the county, is the popcorn capital of the state and host to **Popcorn Days** each September. Call the Chamber of Commerce at (618) 272–7500 for more information. **National Oats Popcorn Factory** is located here.

Two miles off Route 1 and 11 miles south of Cave-in-Rock is Pounds Hollow, an especially scenic recreation area. A twenty-two acre lake is nestled under steep bluffs. Follow Rim Rock Trail around the lake to the prehistoric **Pounds Wall,** a 7,000-year-old Indian structure. It is uncertain whether this Pounds Wall, once 8 to 10 feet high, was used as a fortification or for killing buffalo. Most experts guess the latter use, because a buffalo wallow is nearby. Buffalo would have been rounded up against the wall and slaughtered.

At the southeastern tip of Illinois, on the Ohio River, Hardin County has long been a stopping place for restless pioneers moving west. One of the first was Samuel Mason, an officer of the Continental Army and renegade son of an important Virginia

The Old Slave House

131

family, who came to Illinois territory in 1797. Discovering a deep cavern on the bluff overlooking the river, Mason set himself up in business, advertising over the arched cavern opening, LIQUOR VAULT AND HOUSE OF ENTERTAINMENT. His business, though, was not innkeeping, but rather piracy, and he handily plundered gullible travelers and flatboat crews. When his notoriety caught up with him, he fled, leaving the cave to a long line of fellow thieves. It has gained further fame since being used as a locale for the movie *How the West Was Won* and the two television series about Davy Crockett and Daniel Boone.

Today ❖ **Cave-in-Rock** is part of a state park of the same name, with facilities for picnicking, hiking, boating, fishing, and camping (sixty sites, thirty-five with electric hookups). Off Route 1 and open year-round, Box 338, Cave-in-Rock 62919; (618) 289–4325.

From the little town here runs the only ferry on the Ohio River that shuttles cars and passengers. It operates 6:00 A.M. to 6:00 P.M. daily. On the third weekend in July each year, Cave-in-Rock holds **Frontier Days** to commemorate its historic past. The event features a parade, beauty pageant, carnival, square dancing, and craft exhibits.

Four miles north of Rosiclare near the junction of Route 34 and Route 146 is the **Old Illinois Iron Furnace,** the first in Illinois. It began in 1837 on colorfully named Hog Thief Creek, eventually supporting one hundred families. Some of its production was used at the Mound City Naval Shipyards to clad gunboats during the Civil War. The furnace was abandoned in 1883. There are two interpretive trails at the site along with an inviting "swimming hole" in Big Creek.

At Elizabethtown on Route 146 at the Ohio River is the **River Rose Inn,** (618) 287–8811, a bed-and-breakfast housed in a four-story Greek Revival building. The River Rose Inn specializes in gourmet breakfasts.

Seven miles west from Cave-in-Rock and about 4 miles south of Route 146 is ❖ **Tower Rock Park Recreation Area,** where the scenery is a fine example of that found throughout the Shawnee National Forest, which covers the county. The Ohio River runs along the southern edge of the park, providing opportunities for fishing and boating. Camping and picnicking are also available at Tower Rock. Ranger's Office: (618) 287–2201.

The people of Metropolis will swear to you that Superman really exists. Metropolis claims to be the hometown of the fictional movie and cartoon character Superman. A billboard of Superman welcoming visitors to Metropolis greets you as you enter the town, and another portrait of their hero adorns the water tower. The Chamber of Commerce boasts the only official Superman phone booth, where you can actually speak with the Man of Steel. And just for the sake of continuity, the local newspaper is called the *Daily Planet*.

An annual **Superman Celebration** usually falls on the second weekend in June, runs for two days, and includes a beauty pageant, style show, arts and crafts show, street dance, flea market, and Superman Run.

Metropolis is also the site of the ❖ **Curtis House Museum,** Fourth and Market Streets. This two-story brick house was restored to its original design and is open Sunday from 2:00 to 4:00 P.M. or by appointment. Call (618) 524–5120 for more information.

Old Illinois Iron Furnace

133

Massac County has a historical legend stemming from Fort Massac. One of five former French forts in the Illinois park system, it borders the Ohio River at the southern tip of the state. Indians were believed to have first used the site because of its strategic location on the river. In the early 1540s Spanish explorer Hernando de Soto and his soldiers constructed a fortification here for protection from hostile Indians.

Legend tells us that during the first half of the eighteenth century, many soldiers were massacred here by Indians, thus the name Fort Massacre, later shortened to Massac.

Reconstruction of the fort and an accompanying museum was completed in 1973. Three of the buildings were originally used as living quarters for enlisted men and as means of defense, with loopholes for muskets.

The ◆ **Fort Massac Museum** houses a miniature replica of the fort, artifacts, and a history of the fort. It is open year-round Wednesday through Sunday 10:00 A.M. to 4:30 P.M. Guided tours are available. Call (618) 524–9321 for an appointment.

◆ **Fort Massac State Park** is open daily. The replica of the fort is open 10:00 A.M. to 5:30 P.M. daily. The park offers picnicking, fishing, boating, and camping facilities, and two self-guided trails for hiking. Hunting is allowed in season. For information contact the Site Superintendent, Box 708, Metropolis 62960; (618) 542–9321.

The ◆ **Fort Massac Encampment** is an annual festival recreating the atmosphere of a military encampment in the Illinois country in the 1700s. It is traditionally held the third weekend in October. Contact the park office for events and times.

Fort Massac State Park is located 2½ miles west of Metropolis off I–24 on Route 45. The museum and encampment are on the grounds.

Kitch-mus-ke-nee-be, or the Great Medicine Waters, was once the Indian name for the area known as ◆ **Dixon Springs State Park.** Part of the Illinois Shawnee Hills, the park sits on a giant block of rock, which dropped 200 feet along a fault line that extends northwesterly across Pope County.

The park is about 10 miles west of Golconda on Route 146 near the junction of Route 145. This spot was once occupied by the Algonquin Indians who, after the Shawnee tribe had been driven from Tennessee, settled near the mouth of the Wabash River.

The area was named for William Dixon, one of the first white

134

men to build a home here. He obtained a school land warrant in 1848, and his cabin was a landmark for many years. A small community grew up at Dixon Springs, and in the nineteenth century it became a health spa, which attracted hundreds to the seven springs of mineral-enriched water. A bathhouse provided mineral or soft water baths.

The country is hilly, and during the rainy season rivulets cascade down the hills forming waterfalls.

Picnicking, camping, biking, and hiking are permitted. Enjoy the self-guided 1.7-mile nature trail or the modern swimming pool supplied by spring water, with lifeguard and bathhouse facilities. A concession stand is located near the pool as well as picnic shelters, playgrounds, and drinking water.

The park is open year-round except for holidays. For information contact the Site Superintendent, Dixon Springs State Park, R.R. 1, Brownfield 62911; (618) 949–3394.

The Mansion in Golconda is a Victorian-style house converted into a bed-and-breakfast; (618) 683–4400, P.O. Box 339, Golconda 62938. Full breakfast is included in the fare, and the restaurant is open to the public 11:00 A.M. to 2:00 P.M. and 5:00 to 9:00 P.M. daily except Monday, when it is open 11:00 A.M. to 2:00 P.M. only.

SOUTHWESTERN ILLINOIS

1. Carlyle Lake
2. Eldon Hazlet State Park
3. South Shore State Park
4. Silas Bryan Farm
5. Ingram's Log Cabin Village
6. Stephen A. Forbes State Fish and Wildlife Area
7. Mitchell Museum
8. Cedarhurst Arts Center
9. Rend Lake
10. Wayne Fitzgerrell State Park
11. Southern Illinois University
12. Fern Rocks Nature Preserve
13. Little Grassy Lake
14. Giant City Lodge and Cottages

15. Crab Orchard National Wildlife Refuge
16. Little Grassy Fish Hatchery
17. Buffalo Rock
18. Rainbow Arch
19. Ferne Clyffe State Park
20. *The Hewer*
21. Magnolia Manor
22. Fort Defiance State Park
23. Mound City National Cemetery
24. Thebes Historical Courthouse
25. Trail of Tears State Forest
26. Cobden Museum

SOUTHWESTERN ILLINOIS

THE LAKE REGION

❖ **Carlyle Lake,** the largest inland lake in Illinois, lies primarily within the borders of Clinton County. Created in 1967 by damming the Kaskaskia River, its area covers some 24,580 acres with 83 miles of shoreline. The U.S. Army Corps of Engineers, which maintains the reservoir, estimates that more than 3½ million visitors enjoy the lake each year. Its primary attractions are fishing (for white bass, crappie, largemouth bass, channel catfish, and bluegill), sailing, boating, and hunting, in season. With two state parks on its shore— ❖ **Eldon Hazlet State Park** and ❖ **South Shore State Park**—camping is readily available. More than 400 sites (336 with electric hookup) can be found in the state parks alone. Additional campsites are available at lake recreation areas and at commercial campgrounds. Eldon Hazlet State Park is off Route 127, 6 miles north of Carlyle. South Shore State Park is off U.S. Highway 50, 2 miles east of Carlyle. The parks have the same phone number: (618) 594–3913.

A good place to begin a visit is the **Carlyle Visitor Center,** operated by the U.S. Army Corps of Engineers. The center displays a model of the lake and dam, showing how the reservoir was created. Exhibits of the area's natural history are especially informative. On weekends the center schedules worthwhile interpretive programs such as nature walks, discussions of area Indian history, and water safety seminars. Open Memorial Day through Labor Day 10:00 A.M. to 6:00 P.M. everyday. Open weekends only in May and October; (618) 594–2484. The Carlyle Visitor Center is located at the Dam West recreation area, immediately west of the main dam 1 mile north of Carlyle off Route 127.

The **West Access Marina** supplies services to the lake's boaters—docking and fuel, motorboats, Hobie Cats, sailboards, and cabin sailboats for rent. Rick Golding, the proprietor, can be reached at (618) 594–2461. The marina is immediately west of the main dam, off Route 127 north of Carlyle.

Just south of the main dam, off Route 127, is a 1½-acre plot of natural prairie. In 1974 park rangers seeded the land with grasses and wildflowers indigenous to the Illinois prairie of 150 years ago. A 1-mile trail leads through the prairie. Pick up a walking guide that explains the various plants at the Carlyle Visitor Center.

Carlyle even has its own entry in the National Register of Historic Places—the 1859 **General Dean suspension bridge,** the only suspension bridge in the state. Built to span the Kaskaskia River on the east side of town, the bridge was a link in the old St. Louis–Vincennes Trail. Stone towers 35 feet tall support a 280-foot span. The bridge was restored in 1977 for use as a pedestrian crossing. On the east side of the bridge is a recreation area with picnic tables and grills and a boat ramp. The bridge was named for William F. Dean, a Carlyle native and hero of the Korean War.

The Midwest has few stories about earthquakes, but Salem, surprisingly, was founded as a result of the New Madrid, Missouri, earthquake of 1811. The quake was so powerful that it caused the Mississippi River to flow backwards and sent Capt. Samuel Young in search of a less shaky home. Young came to Marion County and found an abundance of game and tranquility. He even made his camp on what is now the courthouse square in Salem.

Salem became a stagecoach stop on the Vincennes Trail, and the arrival of the railroads in 1850 and 1860 produced Salem's first boom. In the early 1900s oil brought another boom to the town, and in 1939 Salem was the nation's second-largest oilfield.

Salem also has some prominent history in its veins. William Jennings Bryan, called the Silver-Tongued Orator and The Great Commoner, was born here. He was the United States secretary of state, 1913–15, and a three-time presidential candidate. **Bryan's birthplace** is now a museum located near the public library, which also bears his name.

Salem's American Legion Post was a pioneer in producing the GI Bill of Rights. It took seven months and eight days from the time the Salem Legionnaires collaborated on the plan until it was approved by Congress in 1944.

Salem is full of historic architecture, and the Chamber of Commerce, 210 W. Main Street, Salem 62881, (618) 548–3010, has published a walking tour that highlights the sites. The tour begins at North Broadway and Boone Streets and takes you through a **former stagecoach station, Max Corsset's Cafe** (home of Miracle Whip Salad Dressing, which was sold to Kraft Foods in 1931 for $300), past the **Marion County Courthouse,** a **statue of William Jennings Bryan** by Gutzon Borglum (famed sculptor of Mount Rushmore) in the park, and the ◈ **Silas Bryan Farm,** former home of William Jennings Bryan. A separate tour of the home is available. The tour continues on through several homes of the 1800s and 1900s and ends at Bryan's birthplace. Another illustrious native son was the late foorball great Jim Finks, recently inducted into the NFL Hall of Fame.

Other historic sites near Salem are the **One-Room Schoolhouse** located on the Salem Community High School campus, Route 37 North. This one-room schoolhouse has been refurbished to illustrate educational facilities during the nineteenth and early twentieth centuries. It is open 2:00 to 4:00 P.M. on Saturday from April 1 through October, other times by appointment; (618) 548–2799.

The **Halfway Tavern,** 10 miles east of Salem on U.S. Highway 50 East, was built in 1818 and served as a stagecoach stop until 1861. It was built on the trail across Illinois that Capt. George Rogers Clark had used in 1799, and Abraham Lincoln later used it as a stopover.

Ingram's Log Cabin Village

Oil was first discovered near Salem in 1909, but the oil boom came in 1938. The Salem Oilfield ranked seventeenth in the nation in volume of oil production. It currently produces more than 3,000,000 barrels a year. Pumps can be seen at the field 6 miles southwest of Salem.

◆ **Ingram's Log Cabin Village** in Kinmundy, northeast of Salem, has thirteen authentic log buildings dating from 1818 to 1860. Ten of the buildings are authentically furnished and open to the public. The inn is a large, two-story building, once a stagecoach stop. There are several homes, Millican's grocery store and post office, an apothecary, a cobbler's shop, and a church. The village is on sixty-five acres of land with a seven-acre lake.

Hours are by appointment. Contact Ingram's Log Cabin Village, Kinmundy 62854; (618) 547–7123.

The ◆ **Stephen A. Forbes State Fish and Wildlife Area,** 14 miles northeast of Salem, has outdoor recreation including fishing, hunting, boating, picnicking, water-skiing, swimming, camping, hiking, and horseback riding. A **Fisheries Research Center** conducts aquatic biology and fisheries experiments. The center is open to visitors Monday through Friday 7:00 A.M.–4:00 P.M. Tours can be arranged by calling (618) 245–6348.

For information about the park, contact the Site Superintendent, Stephen A. Forbes State Fish and Wildlife Area, R.R. 1, Kinmundy 62865; (618) 547–3381.

Jefferson County is filled with southern hospitality brought over the state line from Dixie. Mount Vernon, the county seat, was settled by southerners and remains peopled by the descendants of southern families.

Mount Vernon is also known as "The King City" because it "crowns southern Illinois."

A variety of activities awaits tourists, ranging from cultural activities to historic sites, to sweet corn and watermelon festivals.

The ◆ **Mitchell Museum,** on the grounds of **Cedarhurst,** an eighty-acre estate, has an 8,000-square-foot exhibit gallery, a smaller lecture gallery, and storage for its extensive collection of nineteenth- and twentieth-century American art acquired by the late John R. and Eleanor Mitchell.

Exhibits specially selected by the Mitchell Museum rotate monthly and include traveling exhibits and annually scheduled shows featuring southern Illinois artists.

To reach the museum, from Broadway turn north at Twenty-seventh Street and then go east on Richview Road to the museum entrance. Museum hours are Tuesday through Saturday 10:00 A.M. to 5:00 P.M. and Sunday 1:00 to 5:00 P.M.; closed Mondays and national holidays. For information call (618) 242–1236.

Cedarhurst has several other attractions including hiking paths, a bird sanctuary, the Cedarhurst Arts Center, and a nineteenth-century restored village. The **Juniper Ridge Trail** is a half-mile path around Mitchell Pond, and the **Braille Trail** has been developed for the sight-impaired. A shelter for bird observation is on the Juniper Ridge Trail.

The ✦ **Cedarhurst Arts Center** contains the county's first jail, a log structure built in 1820, and a log church dating from the 1870s. The Historical Society also has a small museum on the grounds, which is open for special occasions.

Cedarhurst is open Tuesday through Sunday from 8:00 A.M. to 4:00 P.M.; closed Mondays and national holidays. The Arts Center is open Tuesday through Friday 8:00 A.M. to 4:00 P.M. Call (618) 244–6130.

The **Veterans Memorial Walkway** is a memorial to all Jefferson County soldiers killed in war. A special bronze plaque is mounted on granite for each soldier, and these granite stones border the County Courthouse at Route 37 and Main Street in downtown Mount Vernon. An 8-foot-tall black Carmelian granite monolith lists the wars in which Jefferson County citizens participated.

The **Appellate Courthouse** has plenty of history within its walls. Abraham Lincoln successfully argued a famous tax case here in 1859, and Clara Barton used the building as a hospital in 1888. It is now the Fifth District Appellate Court and law library. Tours of the building are available when the court is not in session. It is located at Main and Fourteenth Streets. Hours are Monday through Friday 8:30 A.M. to 4:30 P.M. Call (618) 242–3120 for information.

The newly remodeled **Brehm Memorial Library** houses historical documents regarding local history and genealogy. It is located at 101 South Seventh Street, and its hours are Monday through Thursday 9:00 A.M. to 8:00 P.M., Friday 9:00 A.M. to 5:00 P.M., Saturday noon to 6:00 P.M., and Sunday 1:00 to 5:00 P.M.; (618) 242–6322.

The **Sweet Corn and Watermelon Festival** is held the third week in August. A week of activities includes free sweet corn and watermelon served in the town square. Contact the Mount Vernon Convention and Visitors Bureau, P.O. Box 2580, Mount Vernon 62864; (618) 242–3151.

As well as providing nine to eleven million gallons of water daily for the area, **Rend Lake** provides a recreational retreat. The lake is surrounded by rolling hill prairie country and has excellent crappie fishing. Waterfowl are hunted here as well as deer, rabbit, dove, quail, pheasant, and squirrel.

Picnic grounds for both small and large groups are adjacent to the lake, and **Sleepy Hollow Group Area** is designed for handicapped and disadvantaged youth groups. Advance reservations are necessary for that area.

Beaches are located at the **South Sandusky Recreation Area** and **North Marcum Recreation Area.** There are many boat launching facilities for sailboats and motorboats, and a marina is located on the west side of the lake. An eighteen-hole golf course, tennis courts, pro shop, trap shooting, restaurant, and meeting rooms are also available to tourists.

Observation of geese and ducks, eagles, osprey, loon, swans, heron, and songbirds on the Mississippi Flyway is a special treat for bird-watchers.

For information contact the U.S. Army Corps of Engineers, Rend Lake Management Office, R.R. 3, Benton 62812, (618) 724–2493, or Rend Lake Conservancy District, P.O. Box 497, Benton 62812, (618) 439–4321.

Franklin County shares its greatest natural resource, ❖ **Rend Lake,** with its neighbor, Jefferson County, to the north. Second largest in the state, the 18,900-acre lake has 162 miles of rugged shoreline, next to which is the 3,300-acre ❖ **Wayne Fitzgerrell State Park.** The park has 250 campsites, some with electric hookup, and offers a broad variety of recreational activities. For information contact the Site Superintendent, Wayne Fitzgerrell State Park, Route 154 and I–57, Benton 62812; (618) 629–2320. The park is open year-round.

The Rend Lake Reservoir was created by damming the Big Muddy and Casey Fork Rivers, giving it its unusual Y shape. The Army Corps of Engineers is responsible for the administration of the lake and its visitors center.

Crappie, bass, and catfish are the most-caught species here. In season, hunting is available for all types of waterfowl, quail, pheasant, rabbit, deer, and squirrel.

143

Families will enjoy the picnic areas scattered throughout the lake's recreation areas. The **Sleepy Hollow Group Area** is designed for disadvantaged and handicapped youth (advance reservations necessary). Swimming beaches are located at the South Sandusky and North Marcum recreation areas. The one marina on the west side of the lake has boat rentals available.

On the east side of the lake, the **Rend Lake Golf Course** is a twenty-seven-hole PGA facility with especially scenic terrain. Tennis courts, a restaurant, and a championship trap-shooting range are part of the club. Bird-watching is excellent here, as the lake is situated on the Mississippi Flyway, allowing the observer to view great migrations of geese and ducks and offering sightings of eagles, ospreys, loons, herons, and other birds. In Wayne Fitzgerrell State Park, dog field-trial grounds are host to regional and national championships. For information contact the lake management office; (618) 724–2493. Located on the lake in the state park is **Rend Lake Resort;** (618) 629–2211. This new state facility has cabins and a "boat-el."

In mid-May each year the **Rend Lake Water Festival** features parades, a carnival, craft exhibits, and entertainment. Call (618) 438–2121.

For all of us who love days off, Franklin County's seat, Benton, is where Memorial Day was first established. Here John A. Logan, a Civil War major general, United States representative and senator, and candidate for vice-president in 1884, proposed the holiday in 1868, as commander of the Grand Army of the Republic. A historical marker designates his home site at 204 S. Main Street.

At the southern edge of the county, West Frankfort boasts a fine **Area Historical Museum** on 2000 E. St. Louis Street, with an old one-room schoolhouse, a mines and minerals display, and a program of events such as "Christmas on the Prairie" and "Brides Through the Decades." There's also a branch in the old depot downtown housing veterans' memorabilia. Each September the museum puts on an **"Apple Butter Stir,"** in which the sweet stuff is made in huge copper kettles. It's usually all sold before it's finished cooking! The museum serves a tasty home-style lunch on Wednesday and Thursday from 11:00 A.M. to 1:00 P.M. for only $3.95. It's the best deal going! Museum hours are 9:00 A.M. to 4:00 P.M. Wednesday and Thursday and 1:30 to 4:00 P.M. on Sundays; closed January. Free admission; (618) 932–6159.

Du Quoin got its start as a stopping point on the old Shawneetown-to-Kaskaskia Road, where there was a crossing at the Little Muddy River. The town took its name from Kaskaskia Indian Chief Jean Baptiste Ducoigne, who came to the aid of George Rogers Clark after the fall of Kaskaskia and later served in the Revolutionary Army under Lafayette in Virginia. His tribe camped near the spot of the first white settlement, which took his name. When the railroad came to town in 1853, the town site moved a short distance to its present location.

Today the area is an important center for agriculture and mining and is the largest coal-producing county in Illinois. Numerous strip mines are found throughout the region. Du Quoin's major annual event is the **Du Quoin State Fair,** which begins ten days prior to Labor Day and runs through the holiday. Over 200,000 visitors are attracted to the over-sixty-year-old event. Name entertainment, championship auto racing, and world-class harness racing headline the fair. The fairground's dirt track is called the "Magic Mile" for the number of speed records that have been set here. Tractor pulls and livestock shows round out the schedule. Throughout the year other events are staged at the fairgrounds, including camping rallies and a rodeo. Contact the Du Quoin State Fairgrounds at P.O. Box 191, Du Quoin 62832; (618) 542–9373.

Randolph is one of the most historically and geographically unique counties in all of Illinois. A tiny appendage protruding into the main body of Missouri, Kaskaskia Island is the only part of the state lying *west* of the Mississippi River.

Kaskaskia is the second-oldest settlement (after Cahokia) in the state, founded as a Jesuit mission in 1703. Thus, the area's French heritage is rich. Fort Kaskaskia was erected in the village and served as an outpost in the French and Indian War (1754–63). After the Treaty of Paris in 1763, the region came under British control. In 1778 George Rogers Clark captured the settlement for America, and it became a county of Virginia. It became part of the new Northwest Territory in 1787, part of the Indiana Territory in 1800, the capital of the Illinois Territory in 1809, and the first state capital in 1818 (to 1820 when it moved to Vandalia).

Kaskaskia declined in importance, and Mississippi floods around 1885 eventually destroyed the old settlement, cutting a new channel for the Mississippi through the heart of the town and creating Kaskaskia Island on the western side.

What remained on the eastern side of the river is now **Fort**

Kaskaskia State Historic Site (618–859–3741). The park is an especially scenic area with places for picnicking among the trees. Situated on a hill, it overlooks the Mississippi River and Kaskaskia Island.

Just below the park, at the foot of the hill, between Chester and Ellis Grove, off Route 3, is the **Pierre Menard Home,** now a state memorial. Built in 1802 in French Colonial style, with a wide gallery porch and a low, hipped roof, this was the residence of the first lieutenant governor of Illinois, one of the most important men in the history of the territory. The house has been restored and furnished with pieces of the period. Open daily except major holidays; (618) 859–3031. The museum is free to the public, with hours from 9:00 A.M. to 5:00 P.M.

On **Kaskaskia Island** is the **Liberty Bell of the West.** A gift from Louis XV of France, the bell was towed upriver from New Orleans by men pulling the barge. Today it's a state memorial. To reach the island cross the Chester toll bridge at Route 51 and travel 12 miles to St. Mary's, Missouri, then follow the directional signs to the island.

Chester, the county seat, is the site of **Greenwood Cemetery,** where Shadrach Bond, the first governor of the state (1818–22), is buried. A white granite monument erected by the state in 1883 marks the grave site.

Chester, too, is home to Popeye, the lovable sailorman. His creator, Elzie Crisler Segar, was born here in 1894. In 1977 a **statue of Popeye** was erected in Segar Memorial Park. A **Popeye Picnic and Parade** are usually held the first weekend in September.

North of Chester on Route 3, the Colvis and Gross families have large orchards with peaches, apples, and strawberries for sale. At the **Colvis Orchard,** you can view apple cider being pressed.

Seven miles east of Chester on Route 150 between Chester and Bremen is a **covered bridge** over Mary's River. One of the few such structures in the state, the 98-foot single-span bridge of hand-hewn native oak was erected in 1854.

North of Chester and Fort Kaskaskia are Prairie du Rocher (field of rock) and Fort de Chartres. No missionary is responsible for the settlement here. Instead credit goes to an early entrepreneur who set the stage for a long line of American land speculators to follow. John Law was a Scotch businessman who obtained a charter from

Baldwin

Covered bridge on Mary's River

the French government to colonize the region. His Company of the West brought in immigrants from France, Italy, Switzerland, and Germany. Law promised speculators great profits, but his "Mississippi Bubble" burst in 1720, leaving the settlers stranded.

Most stayed, under the protection of Pierre Duque, Sieur de Boisbriant, commandant of the Illinois country. By 1720 he completed the construction of **Fort de Chartres,** named for the Duc de Chartres, son of the French regent. The fort was rebuilt three times, and its final form was considered one of the strongest in North America.

Today parts of the old fort have been reconstructed and are part of a state park. Each year in June the **Fort de Chartres Rendezvous** creates life in the French era with volunteers in militia uniforms, a fife and drum corps, much firing of canon, and French Colonial cooking. In early October there is an exciting **French and Indian War Encampment.** Fort de Chartres is

147

open year-round, except major holidays, 9:00 A.M. to 5:00 P.M. Admission is free; (618) 284–7230.

In the northwest corner of the county, at Sparta, is the **Charter Oak School,** one of only a few octagonal schoolhouses remaining in the United States. Built in 1873, it served its public purpose until 1953.

From Chester, **U.S. Bicycle Route 76** leads east to Shiloh Hill and the county line, along scenic back roads. Also out in the country is **Kloth's Antiques,** one of the county's better collectible shops, located at the junction of Route 4 and Route 150, 2 miles west of Steeleville.

Perhaps one of the most unusual hotels in the state is the **Original Mineral Springs Hotel and Bath House** in Okawville, just off I–64 in the northwest part of the county. Built in 1892, the forty-room hostelry is listed in the National Register of Historic Places. For more than ninety years, guests have been coming for the relaxing mineral water baths. Book a Swedish massage and a therapeutic soak when you visit. Open year-round: rates for double $42–$85, (618) 243–5458.

The **Okawville Heritage House and Museum** also is listed in the National Register and gives the visitor an idea of life in the last century. Open 1:00 to 4:00 P.M. Monday, Wednesday, and Friday, and noon to 4:00 P.M. Saturday and Sunday.

Nashville is the county seat, named after the hometown of the first settlers from Tennessee. In the northeast part of the city, on thirty-seven acres of rolling wooded land, **Nashville Memorial Park** is a center for outdoor recreational activity. A swimming complex with separate areas for diving, toddlers, and intermediate swimmers was completed in 1981. The pool can accommodate 371 on a busy summer day. The park's other facilities include four baseball diamonds, tennis courts, a playground, picnic areas, and even a challenging par 36 nine-hole municipal golf course.

In town the **First Presbyterian Church,** 300 W. St. Louis Street, is one of the oldest churches in Illinois. Organized in 1832, the present church building dates from 1884.

The **Washington County Historical Society Museum,** 300 S. Kaskaskia Street, houses artifacts and exhibits relative to the history of the area. The museum is open Sunday 1:30 to 3:30 P.M. or by appointment. The historical society also maintains the historic **McKelvey one-room schoolhouse** just west of town (open by appointment only).

Or plan a visit on the third week in September when Nashville holds its yearly **Fall Festival Days** on the courthouse square, complete with music, food, and crafts.

Four miles south of Nashville, off Route 127, is the **Washington County Conservation Area,** a 1,377-acre preserve set in rolling wooded hills. A central part of the area is a 248-acre lake with 13 miles of shoreline. Bass, bluegill, crappie, and catfish are the most frequently caught species. The lake, which has a ten-horsepower limit, has launch ramps and a marina that rents boats and motors and sells tackle, bait, and snacks. A 14-mile trail winds through the woods of the conservation area. Campers, too, can enjoy the habitat, with campsites for tent camping and others with electric hookups and showers. Nine hundred acres are posted for seasonal shotgun and bow-and-arrow hunting. The park is accessible year-round.

THE GREAT OUTDOORS

Carbondale, with a population of 26,000, is the largest city in Jackson County and home to ❖ **Southern Illinois University** (founded in 1869). The college, with 24,000 students, is known for its sports teams, the Salukis, especially in basketball, which is played at SIU Arena, and football, at McAndrew Stadium. If you're in town during the season, be sure to catch a game with all its Southern Illinois enthusiasm. For tickets contact Athletic Ticket Office, SIU, Carbondale 62901; (618) 453–5319. The university's **Faner Museum and Art Galleries** have changing exhibits and works of special interest to southern Illinois. Open daily Tuesday through Saturday 9:00 A.M. to 3:00 P.M., Sunday 1:30 to 4:30 P.M. Call (618) 453–5388.

With the city having a name like Carbondale, one might guess that a primary industry hereabouts is coal mining. On the banks of the Big Muddy River, which flows to the west of Carbondale, was the first coal-mining operation in Illinois. As early as 1810 the river bluffs supplied coal for local needs and to ship downriver to New Orleans. The beauty of the landscape, however, is largely undisturbed, with the Shawnee National Forest beginning just miles to the south and rivers and lakes all around.

Giant City State Park is located in the southeast corner of the county, 12 miles south of Carbondale off U.S. Highway 51 and Route 13 with 3,700 acres of recreational area. The park takes its name from the huge sandstone formations here, such as the dramatic Devil's Stand-table, just west of the park's **Interpretive Center.** The center has trained staff who will explain the various natural features of the park and who present programs on its points of interest.

The **Robinson cabin** in the park is a reconstructed building that depicts life as it was in the area around 1880. An earlier structure, however, is the **Stone Fort,** a prehistoric stone wall at the top of an 80-foot sandstone cliff dating from A.D. 600–900. This is one of ten examples of such forts in southern Illinois, which may have been used for defense or ceremonial purposes.

Other evidence of prehistoric people in the region is found in rock shelters, whose roofs are presumably smoke-stained from campfires. During the Civil War these shelters were used by deserters from both sides.

A surprisingly modern construction in the park is the award-winning design of the park's 100,000-gallon spherical water tank. Eighty-two feet high, the tower has an observation platform with excellent views of the park. Some 50 feet up, the platform is reached by a spiral steel staircase.

Within the park is the 100-acre ❖ **Fern Rocks Nature Preserve,** where such rare plants as French's shooting star and large flowering mint may be found. Hiking is allowed only on the preserve's well-marked trail. Spring may be the best time to visit the park, for it is abloom with more than 170 different types of ferns and flowering plants. Birds abound in the park as well, and they make for excellent bird-watching,

Fishing is offered at ❖ **Little Grassy Lake,** adjacent to the park, and picnicking and camping are available, too (161 sites, 117 with electric hookup). For information on Giant City State Park, contact the Site Superintendent, R.R. 1, Makanda 62958; (618) 457–4836. You will receive a brochure that includes a short discussion of Little Grassy Lake. For a complete list of regulations governing the use of boats on this lake, however, write: Refuge Manager, Crab Orchard National Wildlife Refuge, Marion 62958.

Noncampers will opt for the ❖ **Giant City Lodge and Cottages**—thirty-four rustic cabins built of native stone in the state park. The dining room serves hearty meals around a handsome fireplace. There's a swimming pool here, too. Open February to December; (618) 457–4921.

Jackson County's second major city is Murphysboro, the

county seat. The apple is king here, with more than thirty-one commercial orchards in the vicinity. In fact, mid-September ushers in the annual **Apple Festival,** with pie-baking, apple-peeling and apple-butter contests, a beauty pageant, and a parade led by Captain Applesauce. For dates and events, call the Chamber of Commerce at (618) 684–6421. Historically, Murphysboro claims the birthplace of Gen. John A. Logan, Civil War leader and United States senator.

Lake Kincaid, northwest of Murphysboro, was created in 1972 by the state as a recreation area and water supply for the region. Its 2,750 acres, with 82 miles of timbered shoreline, serve those purposes admirably. Fishing, camping, boating, swimming, and hunting in season are offered. Bass fishing is best during the months of April and May in this deep reservoir, bottoming out at 68 feet near the dam. Lake Kincaid is bounded by Route 149, Route 3, and Route 151 and is located approximately 8 miles west of Murphysboro.

Two marinas service the boating public. One of them, **Southern Illinois Recreation Marina,** not only sells bait and tackle but also has boat rentals, a restaurant, and campground; (618) 687–4914. To get there travel west from Murphysboro on Route 149 approximately 8 miles to a blacktop road marked KINCAID LAKE.

Lake Murphysboro State Park is situated about 1 mile west of Murphysboro off Route 149. The 904-acre park offers a number of recreational possibilities, from fishing to woodland hikes. An unusual feature of the park are patches of native wild orchids. Nine varieties grow here. Camping includes sites with electric hookups (seventy-seven sites total). Contact Site Superintendent, R.R. 4, Murphysboro 62966; (618) 684–2867.

Cedar Lake, in the southern part of the county, is a 1,750-acre body of water only 4 miles south of Carbondale on Route 127.

❦ **Crab Orchard National Wildlife Refuge** was started in the 1930s when the government had rows of pine trees planted to provide work for the WPA (Works Project Administration) and the Civilian Conservation Corps. In 1947 the refuge was officially established by the Department of the Interior and now covers 43,000 acres. The area includes three lakes, twelve natural areas, and a 4,000-acre wilderness area.

Forest, prairie, and wetland plants and animals live harmoniously in Crab Orchard. Wildlife management is centered on providing winter feeding and resting areas for Canada geese, and the refuge's goose flock may build up to 120,000 birds by December. Many species of ducks and bald eagles can be seen in the trees overlooking the goose flock.

Spring brings most of the migratory waterfowl, and eagles, whitetail deer (common year-round), coyote, beaver, muskrat, opossum, and raccoon also inhabit the area. A bird list is available at the refuge headquarters.

Wildlife-oriented recreation is encouraged, and the opportunities for wildlife observation are excellent. For hikers there is the self-guided **Chamnesstown School Trail.** The trail explores a reconstructed schoolhouse and ventures out along old fire trails in open areas of the refuge. Observation towers are wonderful lookouts for watching geese, and there are picnicking areas by **Crab Orchard Lake.**

Hunting and fishing are allowed, and there are a concession-operated campground and marina as well as swimming.

The refuge is located between Carbondale and Marion, accessible from I–57. Visitors are permitted only in designated areas. The visitors center is open 8:00 A.M. to 4:30 P.M. Monday through Friday. For information contact the Project Manager, Crab Orchard National Wildlife Refuge, P.O. Box J, Carterville 62918; (618) 997–3344.

❖ **Little Grassy Fish Hatchery,** downstream of Little Grassy Lake, is a 115-acre hatchery with a visitors' observation area where you can view rearing, spawning, and egg incubation tanks.

The warm-water hatchery combines two methods of fish rearing—intensive and extensive culture. Intensive culture uses a high water exchange through a rearing unit for environmental control and allows rearing of large numbers of fish per unit. Extensive culture uses earthen ponds, an extension of nature, but with some control as to the number of fish per pond and the food organisms available.

The original hatchery was built in 1959, and expansion and modernization began in July 1979, as a result of a state study of projected demands for fish stocking. Largemouth bass, bluegill, redear sunfish, and channel catfish are reared here as well as some smallmouth bass, walleye, muskellunge, northern pike, and striped bass.

The hatchery is southeast of Carbondale and accessible via Little Grassy Road. It is within the boundaries of Crab Orchard

Wildlife Refuge. Visitor tours are on a self-guided basis, though employee-guided tours can be scheduled for large groups. Hours are 8:30 A.M. to 3:30 P.M. daily; (618) 529–4100.

Nearby Marion has a quaint little shopping and dining house called **Collector's Choice,** 500 S. Court Street; (618) 997–4883. Antiques, collectibles, and crafts fill this charmingly decorated Victorian home. A country store takes you back to the era of the well-stocked cracker barrel, and a tearoom features gourmet entrees. Hours for the stores are Monday through Saturday 10:00 A.M. to 5:00 P.M., closed on Sunday. Tearoom hours are 11:00 A.M. to 2:00 P.M. daily, closed on Sunday.

Johnson County is a paradise for those interested in Indian history and nature.

◆ **Buffalo Rock,** 3 miles northeast of Simpson off Route 147 toward Reynoldsburg, has the outline of a buffalo etched into the side of a sandstone cliff. Indians are said to be the artists responsible for this drawing. The trail leading to the site is filled with lovely beech and sugar maple trees, and dozens of colorful wildflowers carpet the forest floor in spring.

The **Milestone Bluff,** north off Route 147 at Robbs, is an ancient Indian dwelling and burial site. The bluff has a prehistoric stone wall and Indian grave sites. The Mississippi Indians are believed to have inhabited the area from A.D. 1000 to 1500. The hiking trail to the bluff begins at the parking lot.

The ◆ **Rainbow Arch,** less than 1 mile west of Cypress off Route 37, is a bridge of sandstone rock surrounded by beautiful white and red oak trees and wild black cherries. One of the largest natural bridges in southern Illinois, it is 66 feet long, 3½ feet wide, and 7 feet high at its peak.

The **River-to-River Trail,** east off U.S. Highway 45, 3½ miles north of I–24 at Vienna, is a dirt trail stretching nearly halfway around the entire southern tip of Illinois. Three connecting trails, make it more than 23 miles long. Plans are being made to extend the trail over the entire southern end of Illinois.

The **Penn Central Tunnel,** 1 mile west off U.S. 45 and 6 miles north of I–24 at Vienna, is one of the oldest stretches of track still in operation. Original construction of the tunnel began in 1871–72 when a tunnel was blasted 800 feet through sandstone and shale. Speed on the track is restricted to 5 miles per hour in the tunnel, 8 miles per hour on the open track. Despite track conditions one train still makes a daily run.

153

The **Little Black Slough Natural Area,** half a mile east of Route 37 and Route 146, is unusual for its terrain. The area is a mixture of primeval tupelo and cypress swamps, rich floodplain forest, and upland woods, with small patches of limestone prairie glades. Some of the oldest living trees east of the Mississippi River are here, and a boardwalk allows access to the heart of the swamp. Nine miles of hiking trails wind through Little Black Slough, and the towering tupelo and cypress trees rising from the swamp make it a unique site in Illinois.

For information about both Little Black Slough Natural Area and the following attraction, contact the Site Superintendent, Ferne Clyffe State Park, P.O. Box 120, Goreville 62939; (618) 995–2411.

♦ **Ferne Clyffe State Park,** 1 mile south of Goreville, has more than 1,000 acres of the largest bluffs and caves in the area. A sixteen-acre fishing lake is within the park. The park has a central valley from which radiate gorges and canyons. Shady dells, natural cathedrals, domes, brooks, cascades, and rills have formed here. Several so-called caves are not really caves but great protruding ledges of rock that make an arched roof.

Hawks Cave is a sheer cliff of stone so hewn by wind and water that an excavation has been made at its base at least 150 feet long and as many feet high. The cave has a natural pulpit and excellent acoustics.

Park facilities include picnicking, fishing, camping, and horseback-riding trails. Call (618) 995–2411 for more information.

Vienna can't live up to the expectations of its name, but it does have some attractions worth seeing. The ***Vienna Times Building*** is beautifully preserved. It was built around 1890 as a bank, and in 1915 the *Vienna Times* newspaper took it over. It is at the Vienna public square 4 blocks west of the junction of Route 146W and U.S. Highway 45 at the corner of East Main and Fourth Streets. It is open to the public during business hours.

The **Paul Powell Home,** also 4 blocks west of this junction at 404 Vine Street, is the home of former Illinois Secretary of State and Illinois Representative Paul Powell. Call (618) 658–4911 for hours. A historical museum is located in the basement of the house.

Cairo, the county seat of Alexander County, is where the magnolia vies with the mimosa. The southernmost city in Illinois, it stands on the tip of a narrow peninsula where the Mississippi and Ohio Rivers join on their journey to the Gulf of Mexico.

This area, known as Little Egypt, has many attractions for tourists to explore. ❧ *The Hewer,* Cairo's art treasure, is a heroic bronze nude by George Grey Barnard. It stands in Halliday Park between Ninth and Tenth Streets. It was presented to the city in 1906 by Mrs. W. P. Halliday and her children in memory of Capt. W. P. Halliday. The statue reads: A VISION OF MEN LABORING ON THE SHORE OF A FLOOD HEWING AND DRAGGING WOOD TO SAVE THE PEOPLE FROM DEATH AND DESTRUCTION. Lorado Taft said *The Hewer* was one of the two finest nudes produced in America.

The **Cairo Public Library** contains several fine works of art. The building itself is an example of Queen Anne architecture. The leaded stained-glass windows are original. In two niches at the entrance stand statues of *Clio,* the Greek muse, and *Concordia,* the Roman goddess of peace. A bronze fountain entitled ***Fishing Boys*** is the work of Janet Scudder, a famous American sculptor.

In the library reference room is a replica of the steamboat ***City of Cairo*** carved by a river pilot, Capt. Henry T. Ashton, in 1876. On the first landing is a rare **Tiffany grandfather's clock,** one of only four of its type made by Tiffany.

Other artifacts are a chandelier originally hung in the Cairo Opera House, a desk belonging to President Andrew Jackson, Cybis porcelains, and a collection of fine paintings.

The library is open from 9:00 A.M. to 5:00 P.M. Monday through Saturday. It is located at 1609 Washington Avenue.

The **U.S. Customs House** at Washington Avenue and Fifteenth Street, is a rare example of a Palazzo or Commercial Italianate-style stone building. There are plans to reopen the building as a Civil War Museum and Cairo Tourism Office.

❧ **Magnolia Manor,** 2700 Washington Avenue, is a Victorian mansion and museum. It is open Monday through Saturday 9:00 A.M. to 5:00 P.M. and Sunday from 1:00 to 5:00 P.M.; (618) 734–0201. The house is a four-story redbrick mansion of Italianate architecture. Large magnolia trees grace its lawn. There are fourteen rooms and a bed slept in by Gen. Ulysses S. Grant.

The **Magnolia Festival** is an annual event that celebrates the blooming of the magnolia trees in Cairo. Dances, concerts, and other activities are held at the Magnolia Manor throughout the first week of May. Contact the Magnolia Manor for information.

Now a park, Fort Defiance, at Cairo Point, was a strategic site for settlement and fortification as early as 1673, when it was first sighted by explorers Jacques Marquette and Robert LaSalle.

Where the Mississippi and Ohio Rivers meet, there is a single piece of mounted artillery. Starting in 1848 the cannon was used to greet arriving boats.

◆ **Fort Defiance State Park** has facilities for picnicking and fishing on its thirty-eight acres. The **Riverboat Memorial** is a triple-decked cement building resembling a square boat. The first deck is a sheltered picnic area with tables. The second and third decks provide outlooks; the second also supports the flagpole. For information contact Park Ranger, Box 77, Miller City 62962; (618) 776–5281.

◆ **Mound City National Cemetery,** 4 miles from the park is a Civil War cemetery with twenty-seven identified Confederate soldiers and 2,441 unknown ones.

The ◆ **Thebes Historical Courthouse** in Thebes, west of Route 3 at Thebes Spur, is a brick and stone courthouse set precariously near the edge of a limestone bluff overlooking the town of Thebes and the Mississippi River. The courthouse was known as the "Courthouse on the Bluff." Here Dred Scott was imprisoned and Abraham Lincoln practiced law. It is an example of Greek Revival architecture and made of local materials. The courthouse is open 10:00 A.M. to 4:00 P.M. daily; (618) 764–2600.

Between mid-December of 1838 and early March 1839, 10,000 Cherokee Indians were forced to travel 800 miles from their home in the Great Smoky Mountains to a reservation in present-day Oklahoma. The exiled Cherokees stopped in southern Illinois because of floating ice on the Mississippi and made camp. The camp provided little shelter against the unusually severe winter that year, and many died. The Cherokee's westward journey became known as the "Trail of Tears."

◆ **Trail of Tears State Forest,** formerly Union State Forest, is northwest of Jonesboro near the Mississippi River. It lies within the beautiful Shawnee Hill country and is a preserve to protect native tree species of Illinois. Approximately sixty acres are devoted to the Union State Tree Nursery, and nearly all species of trees in southern Illinois are found here.

The park has picnicking facilities, approximately forty-four trails totaling more than 36 miles, hunting, and tent camping. You can reach the park by taking Route 3 to Wolf Lake; then drive east for 5 miles. For information call (618) 833–4910.

The **Union County Conservation Area** is in the Lower Mississippi River Bottomlands Division of Illinois. It is a haven for wildlife, most prominent for five months of the year is the flock of Canada geese and other waterfowl that winter in the area. No hunting is allowed, and there are no overnight facilities. This conservation area is southwest of Jonesboro off Route 3 near Reynoldsville. For information contact the Union County Conservation Area, R.R. 2, Jonesboro 62952; (618) 833–5175.

The ◆ **Cobden Museum** in Cobden, affectionately known as the Appleknocker Town, was opened by three amateur archaeologists who spent more than thirty years searching for Indian artifacts in the southern Illinois area. They stored their finds in a basement and soon outgrew the space. Apparently the wives of the amateurs did not like having Indian skeletons and grave goods in their basements and told their husbands to move the stuff. The men decided to open a museum.

Museum hours are weekends only from 12:30 to 4:30 P.M. March through November; (618) 893–2067. It is advisable for visitors to call to make sure the museum is open. It usually closes for the winter in late November and reopens in March. Admission is free, but donations are welcomed.

INDEXES

Entries for Festivals and Museums appear in the special indexes on pages 170–172

Special Indexes

Festivals

Museums

ABOUT THE AUTHORS

Rod Fensom is an author, photographer, and specialist on consumer-travel issues. A former communications manager for Thomas Cook Travel, Fensom has been recognized as a travel expert by *USA Today, Vogue, Time Magazine,* and *U.S. News & World Report.* He has written on travel for *Harpers, Better Homes and Gardens,* the *Chicago Tribune,* and the *Denver Post.* In addition, he has appeared on more than fifty television and radio talk shows—including CBS Evening News—to discuss travel-related topics. Fensom's travels have taken him to China, the former Soviet Union, and countries in Europe, Africa, and South America.

Julie Foreman is a native Chicagoan. She received her master's degree in journalism from Roosevelt University and her bachelor's degree from Northeastern Illinois University. A freelance photographer and travel writer, her articles have appeared in such local publications as the *Chicago Sun-Times, Today's Chicago Woman,* Lerner Newspapers, and Pioneer Press. Along with her extensive exploration of Illinois, Foreman has traveled throughout the United States, Europe, and the former Soviet Union.

Also of Interest from The Globe Pequot Press
Off the Beaten Path Series

These are the fine guides from our Off the Beaten Path series designed for the traveler who enjoys the special and unusual. Each book is by an author who knows the state well, did extensive research, and personally visited many of the places, often more than once. Please check your local bookstore for fine Globe Pequot Press titles, which include:

Alabama	10.95	*Missouri*	10.95
Alaska	11.95	*Montana*	10.95
Arkansas	10.95	*New Hampshire*	10.95
Colorado	10.95	*New Jersey*	10.95
Connecticut	10.95	*New Mexico*	10.95
Florida	10.95	*New York*	10.95
Georgia	10.95	*Northern California*	10.95
Hawaii	12.95	*North Carolina*	10.95
Indiana	10.95	*Ohio*	10.95
Iowa	10.95	*Oregon*	10.95
Kansas	10.95	*Pennsylvania*	10.95
Kentucky	10.95	*Southern California*	10.95
Louisiana	10.95	*Tennessee*	10.95
Maine	10.95	*Texas*	11.95
Maryland	10.95	*Vermont*	10.95
Massachusetts	10.95	*Virginia*	10.95
Michigan	10.95	*Washington*	10.95
Minnesota	10.95	*Wisconsin*	10.95

Available from your bookstore or directly from the publisher. For a free catalogue or to place an order, call toll free, 24 hours a day, 1-800-243-0495, or write to The Globe Pequot Press, P.O. Box 833, Old Saybrook, Connecticut 06475-0833.